VILLAGE-COMMUNITIES

IN THE

EAST AND WEST.

BY THE SAME AUTHOR.

ANCIENT LAW: ITS CONNECTION WITH
THE EARLY HISTORY OF SOCIETY, AND ITS
RELATION TO MODERN IDEAS. 4th Edition,
8vo. 12s.

VILLAGE-COMMUNITIES

IN THE

EAST AND WEST.

SIX LECTURES DELIVERED AT OXFORD

BY

SIR HENRY James SUMNER MAINE, K.C.S.I., LL.D.

CORPUS PROFESSOR OF JURISPRUDENCE IN THE UNIVERSITY;

FORMERLY LAW MEMBER OF THE SUPREME GOVERNMENT OF INDIA.

SECOND EDITION.

LONDON:

JOHN MURRAY, ALBEMARLE STREET.

1872.

LONDON: PRINTED BY
SPOTTISWOODE AND CO., NEW-STREET SQUARE
AND PARLIAMENT STREET

PREFACE.

THE SIX LECTURES which follow were designed as
an introduction to a considerably longer Course, of
which the object was to point out the importance,
in juridical enquiries, of increased attention to the
phenomena of usage and legal thought which are
observable in the East. The writer had not intended
to print these Lectures at present; but it appeared
to a part of his audience that their publication might
possibly help to connect two special sets of investi-
gations, each of which possesses great interest, but
is apparently conducted in ignorance of its bearing
on the other. The fragmentary character of the work
must be pleaded in excuse for the non-performance
of some promises which are given in the text, and
for some digressions which, with reference to the
main subject of discussion, may appear to be of un-
reasonable length.

The eminent German writers whose conclusions

are briefly summarised in the Third and Fifth
Lectures are comparatively little known in England,
and a list of their principal works is given in the
Second Appendix. For such knowledge of Indian
phenomena as he possesses the writer is much in-
debted to the conversation of Lord Lawrence, whose
capacity for the political direction of the natives of
India was acquired by patient study of their ideas
and usages during his early career. The principal
statements made in the text concerning the Indian
Village Communities, have been submitted to Mr.
George Campbell, now Lieut.-Governor of Bengal,
who has been good enough to say that they coincide
in the main with the results of his own experience
and observation, which have been very extensive.
No general assertions are likely to be true without
large qualification of a country so vast as India,
but every effort has been made to control the statements of each informant by those of others.

Some matter has been introduced into the Lectures
which, for want of time, was omitted at their de-
livery.

February 1871.

CONTENTS.

LECTURE I.

THE EAST, AND THE STUDY OF JURISPRUDENCE.

LECTURE II.

THE SOURCES OF INDIAN LAW.

LECTURE III.

THE WESTERN VILLAGE COMMUNITY.

LECTURE IV.

THE EASTERN VILLAGE COMMUNITY.

LECTURE V.

THE PROCESS OF FEUDALISATION.

LECTURE VI.

THE EARLY HISTORY OF PRICE AND RENT.

VILLAGE-COMMUNITIES

IN THE

EAST AND WEST.

———◆———

LECTURE I.

THE EAST, AND THE STUDY OF JURISPRUDENCE.

CONTENTS.

LECTURE I.

THE EAST, AND THE STUDY OF JURISPRUDENCE.

IN the Academical Statute which defines the duties of
the Professor of Jurisprudence, the branches of enquiry to which he is directed to address himself are
described as the investigation of the history and
principles of law, and the comparison of the laws of
various communities. The lectures to which I am
about to ask your attention will deal in some detail
with the relation of the customary law of the East,
and more particularly of India, to the laws and usages,
past and present, of other societies; but, as we are
employed upon a subject—and this is a warning which
cannot be too soon given—in which ambiguities of
expression are extraordinarily common and extremely
dangerous, I perhaps should state at once that the
comparison which we shall be making will not constitute Comparative Jurisprudence in the sense in
which those words are understood by most modern
jurists, or in that which, I think, was intended by the
authors of the statute. Comparative Jurisprudence in
this last sense has not for its object to throw light upon

the history of law. Nor is it universally allowed that
it throws light upon its philosophy or principles.
What it does, is to take the legal systems of two distinct societies under some one head of law—as for
example some one kind of Contract, or the department
of Husband and Wife—and to compare these chapters
of the systems under consideration. It takes the
heads of law which it is examining at any point of
their historical development, and does not affect to
discuss their history, to which it is indifferent. What
is the relation of Comparative Jurisprudence, thus
understood, to the philosophy of law or the determi-
nation of legal principle, is a point on which there
may be much difference of opinion. There is not a
little in the writings of one of the greatest of modern
juridical thinkers, John Austin, which seems to imply
that the authors and expositors of civilised systems
of law are constrained, by a sort of external compul-
sion, to think in a particular way on legal principles,
and on the modes of arriving at juridical results.
That is not my view; but it is a view which may deserve attentive consideration on some other occasion.
It would, however, be universally admitted by competent jurists, that, if not the only function, the chief
function of Comparative Jurisprudence is to facilitate
legislation and the practical improvement of law. It
is found, as matter of fact, that when the legislators
(and I here use the term in its largest sense) of dif-

ferent communities pursue, as they frequently do, the
same end, the mechanism by which the end is at-
tained is extremely dissimilar.   In some systems of
law, the preliminary assumptions made are much
fewer and simpler than in others; the general propositions which include subsidiary rules are much
more concise and at the same time more comprehensive, and the courses of legal reasoning are shorter
and more direct.   Hence, by the examination and
comparison of laws, the most valuable materials are
obtained for legal improvement.   There is no branch
of juridical enquiry more important than this, and
none from which I expect that the laws of our country will ultimately derive more advantage, when it
has thoroughly engrafted itself upon our legal education.   Without any disparagement of the many unquestionable excellences of English law—the eminent
good sense frequently exhibited in the results which
it finally evolves, and the force and even the beauty
of the judicial reasoning by which in many cases they
are reached—it assuredly travels to its conclusions
by a path more tortuous and more interrupted by
fictions and unnecessary distinctions than any system
of jurisprudence in the world.   But great as is the
influence which I expect to be exercised in this country by the study of Comparative Jurisprudence, it is
not that which we have now in hand; and I think it
is best taken up at that stage of legal education at

which the learner has just mastered a very difficult
and complex body of positive law, like that of our
own country. The student who has completed his
professional studies is not unnaturally apt to believe
in the necessity, and even in the sacredness, of all
the technical rules which he has enabled himself to
command; and just then, regard being had to the influence which every lawyer has over the development
of law, it is useful to show him what shorter routes
to his conclusions have been followed elsewhere as
a matter of fact, and how much labour he might
consequently have been spared.

The enquiry upon which we are engaged can only
be said to belong to Comparative Jurisprudence, if
the word 'comparative' be used as it is used in
such expressions as 'Comparative Philology' and
'Comparative Mythology.' We shall examine a
number of parallel phenomena with the view of
establishing, if possible, that some of them are re-
lated to one another in the order of historical succession. I think I may venture to affirm that the Comparative Method, which has already been fruitful of
such wonderful results, is not distinguishable in some
of its applications from the Historical Method. We
take a number of contemporary facts, ideas, and
customs, and we infer the past form of those facts,
ideas, and customs not only from historical records
of that past form, but from examples of it which

have not yet died out of the world, and are still to
be found in it.   When in truth we have to some extent succeeded in freeing ourselves from that limited
conception of the world and mankind, beyond which
the most civilised societies and (I will add) some
of the greatest thinkers do not always rise; when
we gain something like an adequate idea of the vast-
ness and variety of the phenomena of human society;
when in particular we have learned not to exclude
from our view of earth and man those great and
unexplored regions which we vaguely term the East,
we find it to be not wholly a conceit or a para-
dox to say that the distinction between the Present
and the Past disappears.   Sometimes the Past *is* the
Present; much more often it is removed from it
by varying distances, which, however, cannot be
estimated or expressed chronologically.   Direct
observation comes thus to the aid of historical
enquiry, and historical enquiry to the help of direct
observation.   The characteristic difficulty of the
historian is that recorded evidence, however saga-
ciously it may be examined and re-examined, can
very rarely be added to; the characteristic error of
the direct observer of unfamiliar social or juridical
phenomena is to compare them too hastily with
familiar phenomena apparently of the same kind.
But the best contemporary historians, both of
England and of Germany, are evidently striving to

increase their resources through the agency of the
Comparative Method; and nobody can have been
long in the East without perceiving and regretting
that a great many conclusions, founded on patient
personal study of Oriental usage and idea, are vitiated
through the observer's want of acquaintance with
some elementary facts of Western legal history.

I should, however, be making a very idle pre-
tension if I held out a prospect of obtaining, by
the application of the Comparative Method to jurisprudence, any results which, in point of interest or
trustworthiness, are to be placed on a level with
those which, for example, have been accomplished
in Comparative Philology. To give only one reason,
the phenomena of human society, laws and legal
ideas, opinions and usages, are vastly more affected
by external circumstances than language. They are
much more at the mercy of individual volition, and
consequently much more subject to change effected
deliberately from without. The sense of expediency
or convenience is not assuredly, as some great writers
have contended, the only source of modification in
law and usage; but still it undoubtedly is a cause of
change, and an effective and powerful cause. The
conditions of the convenient and expedient are,
however, practically infinite, and nobody can reduce
them to rule. And however mankind at certain
stages of development may dislike to have their

usages changed, they always probably recognise
certain constraining influences as sufficient reasons
for submitting to new rules. There is no country,
probably, in which Custom is so stable as it is in
India; yet there, competing with the assumption
that Custom is sacred and perpetual, is the very
general admission that whatever the sovereign com-
mands is Custom. The greatest caution must therefore be observed in all speculations on the inferences
derivable from parallel usages. True, however, as
this is, there is much to encourage further attention
to the observed phenomena of custom and further
observation of customs not yet examined. To take
very recent instances, I know nothing more striking
among Mr. Freeman's many contributions to our
historical knowledge than his identification of the
fragments of Teutonic society, organised on its
primitive model, which are to be found in the Forest
Cantons of Switzerland. This, indeed, is an example
of an archaic *political* institution which has survived
to our day. The usages which it has preserved are
rather political than legal; or, to put it in another
way, they belong to the domain of Public rather than
to that of Private law. But to usages of this last
class clearly belong those samples of ancient Teutonic
agricultural customs and ancient Teutonic forms of
property in land which Von Maurer has found to
occur in the more backward parts of Germany. I

shall have to ask a good deal of your attention hereafter to the results announced by the eminent writer
whom I have just named; at present I will confine
myself to a brief indication of his method and conclusions and of their bearing on the undertaking
we have in hand.

Von Maurer has written largely on the Law of
the Mark or Township, and on the Law of the
Manor. The Township (I state the matter in my
own way) was an organised, self-acting group of
Teutonic families, exercising a common proprietorship over a definite tract of land, its Mark, cultivating its domain on a common system, and sustaining
itself by the produce. It is described by Tacitus in
the 'Germany' as the 'vicus'; it is well known to
have been the proprietary and even the political unit
of the earliest English society; it is allowed to have
existed among the Scandinavian races, and it survived to so late a date in the Orkney and Shetland
Islands as to have attracted the personal notice of
Walter Scott. In our own country it became absorbed in larger territorial aggregations, and, as the
movements of these larger aggregations constitute
the material of political history, the political historians have generally treated the Mark as having
greatly lost its interest. Mr. Freeman speaks of the
politics of the Mark as having become the politics
of the parish vestry. But is it true that it has lost

its juridical, as it has lost its political importance ? It cannot reasonably be doubted that the Family was the great source of personal law ; are there any reasons for supposing that the larger groups, in which Families are found to have been primitively combined for the purposes of ownership over land, were to anything like the same extent the sources of proprietary law?   So far as our own country is concerned, the ordinary text-books of our law suggest no such conclusion ; since they practically trace our land-law to the customs of the Manor, and assume the Manor to have been a complete novelty introduced into the world during the process which is called the feudalisation of Europe.   But the writings of Von Maurer, and of another learned German who has followed him, Nasse of Bonn, afford strong reason for thinking that this account of our legal history should be reviewed.   The Mark has through a great part of Germany stamped itself plainly on land-law, on agricultural custom, and on the territorial distribution of landed property.   Nasse has called attention to the vestiges of it which are still discoverable in England, and which, until recently, were to be found on all sides of us ; and he seems to me to have at least raised a presumption that the Mark is the true source of some things which have never been satisfactorily explained in English real-property law.

The work of Professor Nasse appears to me to

require some revision from an English professional
lawyer; but, beyond attempting this, I should probably have left this subject in the hands of writers
who have made it their own, if it were not for one
circumstance. These writers are obviously unaware
of the way in which Eastern phenomena confirm
their account of the primitive Teutonic cultivating
group, and may be used to extend it. The Village
Community of India exhibits resemblances to the
Teutonic Township which are much too strong and
numerous to be accidental; where it differs from the
Township, the difference may be at least plausibly
explained. It has the same double aspect of a group
of families united by the assumption of common kinship, and of a company of persons exercising joint
ownership over land. The domain which it occupies
is distributed, if not in the same manner, upon the
same principles; and the ideas which prevail within
the group of the relations and duties of its members
to one another appear to be substantially the same.
But the Indian Village Community is a living, and
not a dead, institution. The causes which trans-
formed the Mark into the Manor, though they may
be traced in India, have operated very feebly; and
over the greatest part of the country the Village
Community has not been absorbed in any larger collection of men or lost in a territorial area of wider
extent. For fiscal and legal purposes it is the pro-

priétary unit of large and populous provinces.   It
is under constant and careful observation, and the
doubtful points which it exhibits are the subject of
the most earnest discussion and of the most vehement controversy.   No better example could therefore be given of the new material which the East, and
especially India, furnishes to the juridical enquirer.

If an ancient society be conceived as a society in
which are found existing phenomena of usage and
legal thought which, if not identical with, wear a strong
resemblance to certain other phenomena of the same
kind which the Western world may be shown to have
exhibited at periods here belonging chronologically
to the Past, the East is certainly full of fragments
of ancient society.   Of these, the most instructive,
because the most open to sustained observation, are
to be found in India.   The country is an assemblage
of such fragments rather than an ancient society
complete in itself.   The apparent uniformity and
even monotony which to the new comer are its most
impressive characteristics, prove, on larger experience,
to have been merely the cloudy outline produced by
mental distance; and the observation of each succeeding year discloses a greater variety in usages and
ideas which at first seemed everywhere identical.
Yet there is a sense in which the first impressions of
the Englishman in India are correct.   Each individual in India is a slave to the customs of the

group to which he belongs; and the customs of the several groups, various as they are, do not differ from one another with that practically infinite variety of difference which is found in the habits and practices of the individual men and women who make up the modern societies of the civilised West. A great number of the bodies of custom observable in India are strikingly alike in their most important features, and leave no room for doubt that they have somehow been formed on some common model and pattern. After all that has been achieved in other departments of enquiry, there would be no great presumption in laying down, at least provisionally, that the tie which connects these various systems of native usage is the bond of common race between the men whose life is regulated by them. If I observe some caution in using that language on the subject of common race which has become almost popular among us, it is through consciousness of the ignorance under which we labour of the multitudinous and most interesting societies which envelope India on the North and East. Everybody who has a conception of the depth of this ignorance will be on his guard against any theory of the development or inter-connection of usage and primitive idea which makes any pretensions to completeness before these societies have been more accurately examined.

Let me at this point attempt to indicate to you the sort of instruction which India may be expected to yield to the student of historical jurisprudence. There are in the history of law certain epochs which appear to us, with such knowledge as we possess, to mark the beginning of distinct trains of legal ideas and distinct courses of practice. One of these is the formation of the Patriarchal Family, a group of men and women, children and slaves, of animate and inanimate property, all connected together by common subjection to the Paternal Power of the chief of the household. I need not here repeat to you the proof which I have attempted to give elsewhere, that a great part of the legal ideas of civilised races may be traced to this conception, and that the history of their development is the history of its slow unwinding. You may, however, be aware that some enquirers have of late shown themselves not satisfied to accept the Patriarchal Family as a primary fact in the history of society. Such disinclination is, I think, very far from unnatural. The Patriarchal Family is not a simple but a highly complex group, and there is nothing in the superficial passions, habits, or tendencies of human nature which at all sufficiently accounts for it. If it is really to be accepted as a primary social fact, the explanation assuredly lies among the secrets and mysteries of our nature, not in any characteristics

which are on its surface. Again, under its best
ascertained forms, the Family Group is in a high
degree artificially constituted, since it is freely re-
cruited by the adoption of strangers.   All this justi-
fies the hesitation which leads to further enquiry; and
it has been strongly contended of late, that by investigation of the practices and ideas of existing
savage races, at least two earlier stages of human
society disclose themselves through which it passed
before organising itself in Family Groups.   In two
separate volumes, each of them remarkably ingenious
and interesting, Sir John Lubbock and Mr. McLennan
conceive themselves to have shown that the first
steps of mankind towards civilisation were taken from
a condition in which assemblages of men followed
practices which are not found to occur universally
even in animal nature,   Here I have only to observe
that many of the phenomena of barbarism adverted
to by these writers are found in India.   The usages
appealed to are the usages of certain tribes or races,
sometimes called aboriginal, which have been driven
into the inaccessible recesses of the widely extending
mountain country on the north-east of India by the
double pressure of Indian and Chinese civilisation, or
which took refuge in the hilly regions of Central and
Southern India from the conquest of Brahminical
invaders, whether or not of Aryan descent.   Many
of these wild tribes have now for many years been

under British observation, and have indeed been administered by British Officers. The evidence, therefore, of their usages and ideas which is or may be forthcoming, is very superior indeed to the slippery testimony concerning savages which is gathered from travellers' tales. It is not my intention in the present lectures to examine the Indian evidence anew, but, now that we know what interest attaches to it, I venture to suggest that this evidence should be carefully re-examined on the spot. Much which I have personally heard in India bears out the caution which I gave as to the reserve with which all speculations on the antiquity of human usage should be received. Practices represented as of immemorial antiquity, and universally characteristic of the infancy of mankind, have been described to me as having been for the first time resorted to in our own days through the mere pressure of external circumstances or novel temptations.

Passing from these wild tribes to the more advanced assemblages of men to be found in India, it may be stated without any hesitation that the rest of the Indian evidence, whencesoever collected, gives colour to the theory of the origin of a great part of law in the Patriarchal Family. I may be able hereafter to establish, or at all events to raise a presumption, that many rules, of which nobody has hitherto discerned the historical beginnings, had

C

really their sources in certain incidents of the Patria
Potestas, if the Indian evidence may be trusted.
And upon that evidence many threads of connection between widely divided departments of law will
emerge from the obscurity in which they have
hitherto been hidden.

But the Patriarchal Family, when occupied with
those agricultural pursuits which are the exclusive
employment of many millions of men in India, is
generally found as the unit of a larger natural group,
the Village Community.   The Village Community
is in India itself the source of a land-law which, in
bulk at all events, may be not unfairly compared
with the real-property law of England.   This law
defines the relations to one another of the various
sections of the group, and of the group itself to the
Government, to other village communities, and to
certain persons who claim rights over it.   The corresponding cultivating group of the Teutonic societies
has undergone a transformation which forbids us to
attribute to it, as a source of land-law, quite the same
importance which belongs to the Indian Village Community.   But it is certainly possible to show that
the transformation was neither so thorough as has
been usually supposed, nor so utterly destructive of
the features of the group in its primitive shape.
When then the Teutonic group has been re-con-
structed by the help of observed Indian phenomena

—a process which will not be completed until both
sets of facts have been more carefully examined
than heretofore by men who are conscious of their
bearing on one another—it is more than likely that
we may be able to correct and amplify the received
theories of the origin and significance of English real-
property law.

Let me pass to another epoch in legal history.
More than once, the jurisprudence of Western Europe
has reached a stage at which the ideas which presided
over the original body of rules are found to have been
driven out and replaced by a wholly new group of
notions, which have exercised a strong, and in some
cases an exclusively controlling influence on all the
subsequent modifications of the law. Such a period
was arrived at in Roman law, when the theory of
a Law of Nature substituted itself for the notions
which lawyers and politicians had formed for themselves concerning the origin and sanctions of the
rules which governed the ancient city. A similar
displacement of the newer legal theory took place
when the Roman law, long since affected in all its
parts by the doctrine of Natural Law, became, for
certain purposes and within certain limits, the Canon
law—a source of modern law which has not yet been
sufficiently explored. The more recent jurisprudence of the West has been too extensive to have
been penetrated throughout by any new theory, but

it will not be difficult to point out that particular
departments of law have come to be explained on
moral principles which originally had nothing whatever to do with them, and that, once so explained,
they have never shaken off the influence of these
principles.   This phenomenon may be shown to have
occurred in India on a vast scale.   The whole of
the codified law of the country—that is, the law contained in the Code of Manu, and in the treatises
of the various schools of commentators who have
written on that code and greatly extended it—is
theoretically connected together by certain definite
ideas of a sacerdotal nature.   But the most recent
observation goes to prove that the portion of the
law codified and the influence of this law are much
less than was once supposed, and that large bodies
of indigenous custom have grow up independently
of the codified law.   But on comparing the written
and the unwritten law, it appears clearly that the
sacerdotal notions which permeate the first have
invaded it from without, and are of Brahminical
origin.   I shall have to advert to the curious circumstance that the influence of these Brahminical theories
upon law has been rather increased than otherwise
by the British dominion.

The beginning of the vast body of legal rules which,
for want of a better name, we must call the feudal
system, constitutes, for the West, the greatest epoch in

its legal history. The question of its origin, difficult enough in regard to those parts of Europe conquered by barbarian invaders which were inhabited by Romanised populations, seemed to be embarrassed with much greater difficulty when it had to be solved in respect of countries like England and Germany Proper, where the population was mainly of the same blood, and practised the same usages, as the conquerors of the Empire. The school of German writers, however, among whom Von Maurer is the most eminent, appears to me to have successfully generalised and completed the explanation given in respect of our country by English historical scholars, by showing that the primitive Teutonic proprietary system had everywhere a tendency, not produced from without, to modify itself in the direction of feudalism; so that influences partly of administrative origin and (so far as the Continent is concerned) partly traceable to Roman law may, so to speak, have been met half-way. It will be possible to strengthen these arguments by pointing out that the Indian system of property and tenure, closely resembling that which Maurer believes to be the ancient proprietary system of the Teutonic races, has occasionally, though not universally, undergone changes which bring it into something like harmony with European feudalism.

Such are a few of the topics of jurisprudence—touched upon, I must warn you, so slightly as to

give a very imperfect idea of their importance and
instructiveness—upon which the observed phenomena
of India may be expected to throw light. I shall
make no apology for calling your attention to a line
of investigation which perhaps shares in the bad
reputation for dulness which attaches to all things
Indian. Unfortunately, among the greatest obsta-
cles to the study of jurisprudence from any point of
view except the purely technical, is the necessity for
preliminary attention to certain subjects which are
conventionally regarded as uninteresting. Every
man is under a temptation to overrate the importance
of the subjects which have more than others occupied
his own mind, but it certainly seems to me that two
kinds of knowledge are indispensable, if the study of
historical and philosophical jurisprudence is to be
carried very far in England, knowledge of India, and
knowledge of Roman law—of India, because it is the
great repository of verifiable phenomena of ancient
usage and ancient juridical thought—of Roman law,
because, viewed in the whole course of its development, it connects these ancient usages and this
ancient juridical thought with the legal ideas of our
own day. Roman law has not perhaps as evil a
reputation as it had ten or fifteen years ago, but
proof in abundance that India is regarded as supremely uninteresting is furnished by Parliament,
the press, and popular literature. Yet ignorance of

India is more discreditable to Englishmen than
ignorance of Roman law, and it is at the same time
more unintelligible in them.   It is more discreditable,
because it requires no very intimate acquaintance
with contemporary foreign opinion to recognise the
abiding truth of De Tocqueville's remark that the
conquest and government of India are really the
achievements which give England her place in the
opinion of the world.   They are undeniably ro-
mantic achievements in the history of a people which
it is the fashion abroad to consider unromantic.
The ignorance is moreover unintelligible, because
knowledge on the subject is extremely plentiful and
extremely accessible, since English society is full of
men who have made it the study of a life pursued
with an ardour of public spirit which would be
exceptional even in the field of British domestic
politics.   The explanation is not, however, I think,
far to seek.   Indian knowledge and experience are
represented in this country by men who go to India
all but in boyhood, and return from it in the maturity of years.   The language of administration and
government in India is English, but through long
employment upon administrative subjects, a technical
language has been created, which contains far more
novel and special terms than those who use it are
commonly aware.   Even, therefore, if the great
Indian authorities who live among us were in perfect

mental contact with the rest of the community, they could only communicate their ideas through an imperfect medium. But it may be even doubted whether this mental contact exists. The men of whom I have spoken certainly underrate the ignorance of India which prevails in England on elementary points. If I could suppose myself to have an auditor of Indian experience, I should make him no apology for speaking on matters which would appear to him too elementary to deserve discussion; since my conviction is that what is wanting to unveil the stores of interest contained in India is, first, some degree of sympathy with an ignorance which very few felicitous efforts have yet been made to dispel, and, next, the employment of phraseology not too highly specialised.

If, however, there are reasons why the jurist should apply himself to the study of Indian usage, there are still more urgent reasons why he should apply himself at once. Here, if anywhere, what has to be done must be done quickly. For this remarkable society, pregnant with interest at every point, and for the moment easily open to our observation, is undoubtedly passing away. Just as according to the Brahminical theory each of the Indian sacred rivers loses in time its sanctity, so India itself is gradually losing everything which is characteristic of it. I may illustrate the completeness of the trans-

formation which is proceeding by repeating what I
have learned, on excellent authority, to be the opinion
of the best native scholars: that in fifty years all
knowledge of Sanscrit will have departed from India,
or, if kept alive, will be kept alive by the reactive
influence of Germany and England.   Such assertions
as these are not inconsistent with other statements
which you are very likely to have heard from men
who have passed a life in Indian administration.
Native Indian society is doubtless as a whole very
ignorant, very superstitious, very tenacious of usages
which are not always wholesome.   But no society in
the world is so much at the mercy of the classes
whom it regards as entitled by their intellectual or
religious cultivation to dictate their opinions to others,
and a contagion of ideas, spreading at a varying rate
of progress, is gradually bringing these classes under
the dominion of foreign modes of thought.   Some of
them may at present have been very slightly affected
by the new influence; but then a comparatively slight
infusion of foreign idea into indigenous notions is
often enough to spoil them for scientific observation.
I have had unusual opportunities of studying the
mental condition of the educated class in one Indian
province.   Though it is so strongly Europeanised
as to be no fair sample of native society taken as a
whole, its peculiar stock of ideas is probably the
chief source from which the influences proceed which

are more or less at work everywhere. Here there
has been a complete revolution of thought, in literature, in taste, in morals, and in law.   I can only
compare it to the passion for the literature of Greece
and Rome which overtook the Western world at the
revival of letters; and yet the comparison does not
altogether hold, since I must honestly admit that
much which had a grandeur of its own is being replaced by a great deal which is poor and ignoble.
But one special source of the power of Western ideas
in India I mention with emphasis, because it is not
as often recognised as it should be, even by men of
Indian experience.   These ideas are making their
way into the East just at the period when they are
themselves strongly under the influence of physical
knowledge, and of the methods of physical science.
Now, not only is all Oriental thought and literature
embarrassed in all its walks by a weight of false
physics, which at once gives a great advantage to all
competing forms of knowledge, but it has a special
difficulty in retaining its old interest.   It is elabo-
rately inaccurate, it is supremely and deliberately
careless of all precision in magnitude, number, and
time.   But to a very quick and subtle-minded people,
which has hitherto been denied any mental food but
this, mere accuracy of thought is by itself an intellectual luxury of the very highest order.

It would be absurd to deny that the disintegration

of Eastern usage and thought is attributable to British
dominion.   Yet one account of the matter which is
very likely to find favour with some Englishmen and
many foreigners is certainly not true, or only true
with the largest qualifications.   The interference of
the British Government has rarely taken the form of
high-handed repression or contemptuous discourage-
ment.   The dominant theory has always been that
the country ought to be governed in conformity with
its own notions and customs; but the interpretation
of these notions and customs has given rise to the
widest differences of opinion, and it is the settled
habit of the partisans of each opinion to charge their
adversaries with disregard of native usage.   The
Englishman not personally familiar with India
should always be on his guard against sweeping
accusations of this sort, which often amount in reality
to no more than the imputation of error on an
extremely vague and difficult question, and possibly
a question which is not to be solved by exclusively
Indian experience.   If I were to describe the feeling
which is now strongest with some of the most ener-
getic Indian administrators, I should be inclined to
call it a fancy for reconstructing native Indian society
upon a purely native model ; a fancy which some
would apparently indulge, even to the abnegation of
all moral judgment.   But the undertaking is not
practicable.   It is by its indirect and for the most

part unintended influence that the British power metamorphoses and dissolves the ideas and social forms underneath it; nor is there any expedient by which it can escape the duty of rebuilding upon its own principles that which it unwillingly destroys.

LECTURE II.

THE SOURCES OF INDIAN LAW.

CONTENTS.

LECTURE II.

THE SOURCES OF INDIAN LAW.

CONTENTS.

LECTURE II.

THE SOURCES OF INDIAN LAW.

THE bodies of customary law which exist in India have now and then been more or less popularly described by acute observers who were led to examine them by curiosity or official duty; but on the whole the best information we possess concerning native usage is that which has been obtained through judicial or quasi-judicial agency. The agency which I have here called 'quasi-judicial' belongs to a part of Anglo-Indian administration which is very little understood by Englishmen, but which is at the same time extremely interesting and instructive. Its origin and character may be described as follows— inadequately no doubt, but still without substantial inaccuracy.

The British Government, like all Eastern sovereigns, claims a large share of the produce of the soil, most of which, however, unlike other Eastern sovereigns, it returns to its subjects through the judicial and administrative services which it maintains, and through the public works which it systematically executes. Some person, or class of persons, must of course be responsible to it for the due payment of this 'land-revenue,' and this person or class must have the power of collecting it from the other owners and cultivators of the soil. This double necessity, of determining the persons immediately responsible for its share of the profits of cultivation and of investing them with corresponding authority, has involved the British Indian Government, ever since the very infancy of its dominion, in what I believe to be the most arduous task which a government ever undertook. It has had not only to frame an entire law of land for a strange country, but to effect a complete register of the rights which the law confers on individuals and definite classes. When a province is first incorporated with the Empire, the first step is to effect a settlement or adjustment of the amount of rent claimable by the State. The functionaries charged with this duty are known as the Settlement Officers. They act under formal instructions from the provincial government which has deputed them; they communicate freely with it during their enquiries; and they wind them up with a Settlement Report, which is often a most comprehensive account of the new province, its history, its natural products, and above all the usages of its population. But the most important object of the Settlement operations—not second even to the adjustment of the Government revenues—is to construct a ' Record of Rights,' which is a detailed register of all rights over the soil in the form in which they are believed to have existed on the eve of the conquest or annexation. Here it is that the duties of the Settlement Officers assume something of a judicial character. The persons who complain of any proposed entry on the register may insist on a formal hearing before it is made.

When the Record of Rights has been completed and the amount of Government revenue has been adjusted, the functions of the Settlement Officers are at an end, and do not revive until the period is closed for which the Settlement has been made. But, during the currency of this period, questions between the State and the payer of land-tax still continue to arise in considerable number, and it is found practically impossible to decide on such questions without occasionally adjudicating on private rights. Another quasi-judicial agency is therefore that of the functionaries who, individually or collectively, have jurisdiction in such disputes, and who are variously known as Revenue Officers, Revenue Courts, and Revenue Boards—expressions extremely apt to mislead the Englishman unused to Indian official documents. The Circulars and Instructions issued by their superiors to Settlement and Revenue officers, their Reports and

D

. decisions on disputed points, constitute a whole literature of very great extent and variety and of the
utmost value and instructiveness. I am afraid I
must add that the English reader, whose attention is
not called to it by official duty, not unusually finds
it very unattractive or even repulsive. But the
reason I believe to be that the elementary knowledge
which is the key to it has for the most part never
been reduced to writing at all.

So far as the functions of the Settlement and
Revenue Officers constitute a judicial agency, the
jurisdiction exercised by them was at first established by the British Government not in its character
of sovereign, but in its capacity of supreme landowner. It was merely intended to enforce the
claim of the State with some degree of regularity and
caution. The strictly judicial agency of which I
spoke is that of the Civil Courts, which are very
much what we understand in this country by ordinary Courts of Justice. Theoretically, whenever the
Settlement or Revenue Courts decide a question of
private right, there is almost always (I need not
state the exceptions) an appeal from their decision to
the Civil Courts. Yet, taking India as a whole,
these appeals are surprisingly few in comparison
with the cases decided. This is one of the reasons
why the literature of Settlement and Revenue operations is a fuller source of information concerning the

customs of ownership and tenure observed among
the natives of India than the recorded decisions of
the Civil Courts.

Yet, though the results of quasi-judicial agency in
India are, on the whole, more instructive than the
results of strictly judicial agency, the Indian Civil
Courts have nevertheless been largely instrumental
in bringing into light the juridical notions peculiar
to the country, in contrasting them with the legal
ideas of the Western World, and to a certain extent
in subjecting them to a process of transmutation.
For reasons which will appear as I proceed, it is
desirable that I should give you some account of
these courts. I will endeavour to do it briefly and
only in outline.

All India at the present moment, with the exception of the most unsettled provinces, is under the
jurisdiction of five High or Chief Courts. The difference between a High and Chief Court is merely
technical, one being established by the Queen's
Letters Patent, under an Act of Parliament, the
other by an enactment of the Indian Legislature. Of
these courts, three are considerably older than the
rest, and are in fact almost as old as the British
dominion in India. When, however, the texture of
the jurisdiction of the High Courts which sit at
Calcutta, Madras, and Bombay, is examined, it is
seen to consist of two parts, having a different

history. An Indian lawyer expresses this by saying that the three older High Courts were formed by the fusion of the 'Supreme' and 'Sudder' Courts, words which have the same meaning but which indicate very different tribunals.

The Supreme Courts, invested with special judicial powers over a limited territory attached to the three old fortified factories of the East India Company at Calcutta, Madras, and Bombay—or, as they were once called, and are still called officially, Fort William, Fort St. George, and Bombay Castle—may be shortly described as three offshoots from Westminster Hall planted in India. They were 'Courts of Record, exercising Civil, Criminal, Admiralty, and Ecclesiastical jurisdiction,' and their judges were barristers taken straight from the English Bar. Although a series of statutes and charters provided securities for the application of native law and usage to the cases of their native suitors, and though some of the best treatises on Hindoo law which we possess were written by Supreme Court judges, it would not be incorrect to say that on the eve of the enactment of the several Indian Codes, the bulk of the jurisprudence administered by the Supreme Courts consisted of English law, administered under English procedure. Lord Macaulay, in the famous essay on Warren Hastings, has vividly described the consternation which the most important of these courts

caused in its early days among the natives subject to
its power; and there is no doubt that the establishment of a tribunal on similar principles would now-
a-days be regarded as a measure of the utmost
injustice and danger. Yet there is something to be
said in mitigation of the condemnation which the
Supreme Courts have received everywhere except in
India. The great quantity of English law which had
worked its way into their jurisprudence is doubtless
to be partially accounted for by the extravagant
estimate universally set by English lawyers upon
their own system, until their complacency was rudely
disturbed by Bentham; but at the same time the
apparently inevitable displacement of native law and
usage by English law, when the two sets of rules are
in contact, is a phenomenon which may be observed
over a great part of India at the present moment.
The truth is that the written and customary law of
such a society as the English found in India is not of
a nature to bear the strict criteria applied by English
lawyers. The rule is so vague as to seem capable
of almost any interpretation, and the construction
which in those days an English lawyer would place
on it, would almost certainly be coloured by associations collected from English practice. The strong
statements, too, which have been made concerning
the unpopularity of these courts on their first
establishment must be received with some caution.

Unquestionably great and general dismay was caused
by their civil procedure, conferring as it did powers
of compelling the attendance of witnesses, and of
arresting defendants both before and after judgment,
which were quite foreign to the ideas of the country.
There were constant complaints, too, of the application of the English law of forgery to India.   It is
true that, as regards the case which Lord Macaulay
has sketched with such dramatic force, Nuncomar
appears to me, upon the records of the proceedings,
to have had quite as fair a trial as any Englishman
of that day indicted for forgery would have had in
England, and to have been treated with even more
consideration by the Court.   But the introduction of
the law under which he suffered was felt as a general
grievance, and there are many representations on
the subject in the archives of the Indian Government.
These archives, however, which have been recently
examined, and in part published, seem to me to prove
that the native citizens of Calcutta, so far from com-
plaining of the civil law imported by the Supreme
Court from Westminster Hall and of the bulk of the
criminal law, actually learned to echo the complacent
encomiums on its perfection which they heard from
English Judges.   The fact appears to me so well
established that I venture to draw some inferences
from it.   One is of a political nature, and need not
be dwelt on here.   A nervous fear of altering native

custom has, ever since the terrible events of 1857, taken possession of Indian administrators; but the truth is the natives of India are not so wedded to their usages that they are not ready to surrender them for any tangible advantage, and in this case the even justice of these courts was evidently regarded as quite making up for the strangeness of the principles upon which they acted. Another conclusion is of more direct importance to the jurist. Complete and consistent in appearance as is the codified law of India, the law enunciated by Manu and by the Brahminical commentators on him, it embraces a far smaller portion of the whole law of India than was once supposed, and penetrates far less deeply among the people. What an Oriental is really attached to is his local custom, but that was felt to have been renounced by persons taking refuge at a distance from home, under the shelter of the British fortresses.

The chief interest of these Supreme Courts to the student of comparative jurisprudence arises from the powerful indirect influence exerted by them on the other courts which I mentioned, and with which eight years ago they were combined—the Sudder Courts. Nevertheless, some of the questions which have incidentally come before the Supreme Courts, or before the branch of the High Court which continues their jurisdiction, have thrown a good deal of light on the mutual play of Eastern and Western legal thought in the British Indian Empire. The judges who presided over the most important of these courts very early recognised the existence of testamentary power among the Hindoos. It seems that, in the province of Lower Bengal, where the village-system had been greatly broken up, the head of the household had the power of disposing of his patrimony during life. Whether he could dispose of it at death, and thus execute a disposition in any way resembling a will, has always been a much disputed question — which, however, contemporary opinion rather inclines towards answering in the negative. However that may be, the power of making a will was soon firmly established among the Hindoos of Lower Bengal by, or through the influence of, the English lawyers who first entered the country. For a long time these wills, never very frequently used, were employed, as the testaments of Roman citizens can be shown to have been employed, merely to supplement the arrangements which, without them, would have been made by the law of intestate succession. But the native lawyers who practise in Calcutta live in an atmosphere strongly charged with English law, and wills drafted by them or at their instance, and exactly resembling the will of a great English landed proprietor, were coming in increasing numbers before the Courts, up to the time when the

law of testamentary succession was finally simplified
and settled by a recent enactment of the Indian
Legislature. In such wills the testator claimed to
arrange a line of succession entirely for himself,
not only providing for the enjoyment of the property
by his descendants in such order as he pleased, but
even excluding them, if he liked, altogether from the
succession; and, in order to obtain his object, he also
necessarily claimed to have the benefit of a number
of fictions or artificial notions, which made their way
into English law from feudal and even from scho-
lastic sources. The most interesting of these wills
was executed by a Brahmin of high lineage who
made a fortune at the Calcutta Bar, and he aimed
at disinheriting or excluding from the main line of
succession a son who had embraced Christianity.
The validity and effect of the instrument have yet to
be declared by the Privy Council; and all I can say
without impropriety is that, in those parts of India
in which the collective holding of property has not
decayed as much as it has done in Lower Bengal,
the liberty of testation claimed would clearly be
foreign to the indigenous system of the country.
That system is one of common enjoyment by village-
communities, and, inside those communities, by
families. The individual here has almost no power
of disposing of his property; even if he be chief of
his household, the utmost he can do, as a rule, is to

regulate the disposition of his property among his
children within certain very narrow limits.   But the
power of free testamentary disposition implies the
greatest latitude ever given in the history of the
world to the volition or caprice of the individual.
Independently, however, of all questions of substance,
nothing could be more remarkable than the form of
the will which I spoke of as having fallen under
the jurisdiction of the tribunal which now represents
the Supreme Court of Calcutta.   Side by side by
recitals, apparently intended to conceal the breach
in the line of descent, by affirming that the testator had, while living, made suitable provision for
the disinherited son, were clauses settling certain
property in perpetuity on the idols of the family,
and possibly meant to propitiate them for the irregu-
larity in the performance of the *sacra* which the new
devolution of the inheritance inevitably entailed.
The testator formally stated that he and his brothers
had failed in business, that all the property they had
inherited had been lost in the disaster, and that the
fortune of which he was disposing was acquired by
his individual exertions.   This was meant to take the
funds with which the will dealt out of the Hindoo
family system and to rebut the presumption that the
gains of a brother belonged to the common stock
of the joint family.   But these provisions referring
to Hindoo joint property were followed by others

creating joint estates on the English model; and here the testator employed legal terms only capable of being thoroughly understood by a person familiar with that extraordinary technical dialect expressing the incidents of joint-tenancy which the fathers of English law may be seriously suspected of having borrowed from the Divinity Schools of Oxford and Cambridge.

The other court which has been recently combined with the court I have been describing, retained to the last its native name of Sudder Court. It underwent some changes after its first establishment, but it may be roughly said to date from the assumption by the English of territorial sovereignty. When finally organised, it became the highest court of appellate jurisdiction from all the courts established in the territories dependent on the seat of government, saving always the Supreme Court, which had exclusive jurisdiction within the Presidency Town, or (as it might be called) the English metropolis. The nature of the local tribunals from which an appeal lay to the Sudder Court is a study by itself; and I must content myself with stating that the Indian judicial system at present resembles not the English but the French system; that a number of local courts are spread over the country, from each of which an appeal lies to some higher court, of which the decisions are again appealable to the court,

whether called Sudder or High Court, which stands
at the apex.   The Sudder Courts therefore decided in
the last resort questions arising originally at some point
or other of a vast territory, a territory in some cases
containing a population equal to that of the largest
European States.   Except the Indian Settlement
and Revenue Courts which I began this Lecture
by describing, no tribunal in the world has ever had
to consider a greater variety of law and usage.

What that law and usage was, the Sudder Court
used to ascertain with what some would call most
conscientious accuracy and others the most technical
narrowness.   The judges of the Court were not
lawyers, but the most learned civilians in the service
of the East India Company, some of whom have left
names dear to Oriental learning.   They were strongly
influenced by the Supreme Court which sat in their
neighbourhood; but it is curious to watch the different effect which the methods of English law had
on the two tribunals.   At the touch of the Judge of
the Supreme Court, who had been trained in the
English school of special pleading, and had probably
come to the East in the maturity of life, the rule of
native law dissolved and, with or without his intention, was to a great extent replaced by rules having
their origin in English law-books.   Under the hand
of the Judges of the Sudder Courts, who had lived
since their boyhood among the people of the country,

the native rules hardened, and contracted a rigidity
which they never had in real native practice. The
process was partly owing to their procedure, which
they seem to have borrowed from the procedure of the
English Court of Chancery, at that time a proverb at once
of complexity and technical strictness. It has been
said by an eminent Indian lawyer that, when the Judges
of the Sudder Courts were first set to administer native
law, they appear to have felt as if they had got into
fairyland, so strange and grotesque were the legal principles on which they were called to act. But after
a while they became accustomed to the new region,
and began to behave themselves as if all were real
and substantial. As a matter of fact, they acted as
if they believed in it more than did its native inhabi-
tants. Among the older records of their proceedings
may be found injunctions, couched in the technical
language of English Chancery pleadings, which forbid the priests of a particular temple to injure a rival
fane by painting the face of their idol red instead of
yellow, and decrees allowing the complaint of other
priests that they were injured in property and repute
because their neighbours rang a bell at a particular
moment of their services. Much Brahminical ritual
and not a little doctrine became the subject of decision. The Privy Council in London was once
called upon to decide in ultimate appeal on the claims
of rival hierophants to have their palanquin carried

cross-wise instead of length-wise; and it is said that
on another occasion the right to drive elephants
through the narrow and crowded streets of one of
the most sacred Indian cities, which was alleged to
vest in a certain religious order as being in possession
of a particular idol, was seriously disputed because
the idol was cracked.

There is in truth but little doubt that, until education began to cause the natives of India to absorb
Western ideas for themselves, the influence of the
English rather retarded than hastened the mental
development of the race. There are several departments of thought in which a slow modification of
primitive notions and consequent alteration of practice may be seen to have been proceeding before we
entered the country; but the signs of such change are
exceptionally clear in jurisprudence, so far, that is
to say, as Hindoo jurisprudence has been codified.
Hindoo law is theoretically contained in Manu, but
it is practically collected from the writings of the
jurists who have commented on him and on one
another. I need scarcely say that the mode of developing law which consists in the successive com-
ments of jurisconsult upon jurisconsult, has played
a very important part in legal history. The middle
and later Roman law owes to it much more than to
the imperial constitutions; a great part of the Canon
law has been created by it; and, though it has been

a good deal checked of late years by the increased activity of formal legislatures, it is still the principal agency in extending and modifying the law of continental countries.   It is worth observing that it is on the whole a liberalising process.   Even so obstinate a subject-matter as Hindoo law, was visibly changed by it for the better.   No doubt the dominant object of each successive Hindoo commentator is so to construe each rule of civil law as to make it appear that there is some sacerdotal reason for it; but, subject to this controlling aim, each of them leaves in the law after he has explained it, a stronger dose of common sense and a larger element of equity and reasonableness than he found in it as it came from the hands of his predecessors.

The methods of interpretation which the Sudder Courts borrowed from the Supreme Courts and which the Supreme Courts imported from Westminster Hall, put a stop to any natural growth and improvement of Hindoo law.   As students of historical jurispudence, we may be grateful to them for it; but I am clearly persuaded that, except where the Indian Legislature directly interfered—and of late it has interfered rather freely,—the English dominion of India at first placed the natives of the country under a less advanced regimen of civil law than they would have had if they had been left to themselves.   The phenomenon seems to me one of considerable interest to the jurist. Why is it that the English mode of developing law by decided cases tends less to improve and liberalise it than the interpretation of written law by successive commentators? Of the fact there seems no question. Even where the original written law is historically as near to us as are the French Codes, its development by text-writers is on the whole more rapid than that of English law by decided cases. The absence of any distinct check on the commentator and the natural limitations on the precision of language are among the causes of the liberty he enjoys; so also is the power which he exercises of dealing continuously with a whole branch of law; and so too are the facilities for taking his own course afforded him by inconsistencies between the dicta of his predecessors—inconsistencies which are so glaring in the case of the Hindoo lawyers, that they were long ago distributed into separate schools of juridical doctrine. The reason why a Bench of Judges, applying a set of principles and distinctions which are still to a great extent at large, should be as slow as English experience shows them to be in extension and innovation, is not at first sight apparent. But doubtless the secret lies in the control of the English Bench by professional opinion—a control exerted all the more stringently when the questions brought before the courts are merely insulated fragments of particular branches of law. English law is, in fact, confided to the custody of a great corporation, of which the Bar, not the Judges, are far the largest and most influential part. The majority of the corporators watch over every single change in the body of principle deposited with them, and rebuke and practically disallow it, unless the departure from precedent is so slight as to be almost imperceptible.

Let us now consider what was the law which, under the name of native custom, the courts which I have been describing undertook to administer. I shall at present attend exclusively to the system which, as being the law of the enormous majority of the population, has a claim to be deemed the common-law of the country—Hindoo law. If I were technically describing the jurisdiction, I should have to include Mahometan law, and the very interesting customs of certain races who have stood apart from the main currents of Oriental conquest and civilisation, and are neither Mahometan nor Hindoo. Mahometan law, theoretically founded on the Koran, has really more interest for the jurist than has sometimes been supposed, for it has absorbed a number of foreign elements, which have been amalgamated by a very curious process with the mass ot semi-religious rules ; but the consideration of this may conveniently be postponed, as also the discussion of the outlying bodies of non-Hindoo usage found in various parts of the country.

E

The Hindoo law, then, to which the English in India first substantially confined their attention, consisted, first, of the Institutes of Manu, pretending to a divine inspiration, of which it is not easy to define the degree and quality, and, next, of the catena of commentators belonging to the juridical school admitted to prevail in the province for which each particular court was established. The Court did not in early times pretend to ascertain the law for itself, but took the opinion of certain native lawyers officially attached to the tribunal. But from the first there were some specially learned Englishmen on the bench who preferred to go for themselves to the fountains of law, and the practice of consulting the ' Pundits ' was gradually discontinued. These Pundits laboured long under the suspicion, to a great degree unmerited, of having trafficked with their privilege, and having often, from corrupt motives, coined the law which they uttered as genuine. But the learned work of Mr. West and Professor Bühler, following on other enquiries, has gone far to exonerate them, as the greater part of their more important opinions have been traced to their source in recognised authorities. That they were never corrupt it is unfortunately never safe to affirm of Orientals of their time; but their opportunity was probably taken from the vagueness of the texts which they had to interpret. There are in fact certain dicta of Hindoo authoritative commentators upon which almost any conclusion could be based.

The codified or written law of the Hindoos, then assumed to include their whole law, consisted of a large body of law regulating the relations of classes, especially in the matter of intermarriage; of a great body of family law, and a correspondingly extensive law of succession; and of a vast number of rules regulating the tenure of property by joint families, the effects on proprietary right of the division of those families, and the power of holding property independently of the family. There was some law of Contract and some law of Crime ; but large departments of law were scantily represented, or not at all, and there was in particular a singular scarcity of rules relating specially to the tenure of land, and to the mutual rights of the various classes engaged in its cultivation. This last peculiarity was all the more striking because the real wealth of the country is, and always has been, agricultural, and the religious and social customs of the people, even as recorded in the codified law, savour strongly of agriculture as their principal occupation.

It would-seem that doubts as to the relation of the codified or written law to the totality of native usage were entertained at a very early time, and collections were made of local rules which applied to the very points discussed by the Brahminical jurists,

and yet disposed of them in a very different manner.
These doubts have steadily gained strength.   I
think I may venture to lay down generally, that the
more exclusively an Anglo-Indian functionary has
been employed in ' revenue ' administration, and the
further removed from great cities has been the scene
of his labours, the greater is his hesitation in admit-
ting that the law assumed to begin with Manu is, or
ever has been, of universal application.   I have also
some reason to believe that the Judges of the newest
of the High Courts, that established a few years
ago for the provinces of the North-West in which
primitive usage was from the first most carefully
observed and most respected, are of opinion that they
would do great injustice if they strictly and uniformly
administered the formal written law.   The conclusion
arrived at by the persons who seem to me of highest
authority is, *first*, that the codified law—Manu and
his glossators—embraced originally a much smaller
body of usage than had been imagined, and, *next*,
that the customary rules, reduced to writing, have
been very greatly altered by Brahminical expositors,
constantly in spirit, sometimes in tenor.   Indian law
may be in fact affirmed to consist of a very great
number of local bodies of usage, and of one set of
customs, reduced to writing, pretending to a diviner
authority than the rest, exercising consequently a
great influence over them, and tending, if not checked,

to absorb them. You must not understand that these bodies of custom are fundamentally distinct. They are all marked by the same general features, but there are considerable differences of detail; and the interest of these differences to the historical jurist is very great, for it is by their help that he is able chiefly to connect the customs of India with what appear to have been some of the oldest customs of Europe and the West.

As you would expect, the written law, having been exclusively set forth and explained by Brahmins, is principally distinguished from analogous local usages by additions and omissions for which sacerdotal reasons may be assigned. For instance, I have been assured from many quarters that one sweeping theory, which dominates the whole codified law, can barely be traced in the unwritten customs. It sounds like a jest to say that, according to the principles of Hindoo law, property is regarded as the means of paying a man's funeral expenses, but this is not so very untrue of the written law, concerning which the most dignified of the Indian Courts has recently laid down, after an elaborate examination of all the authorities, that ' the right of inheritance, according to Hindoo law, is wholly regulated with reference to the spiritual benefits to be conferred on the deceased proprietor.' There are also some remarkable differences between the written and unwritten law in

their construction of the rights of widows. That
the oppressive disabilities of widows found in modern Hindoo law, and especially the prohibition of
re-marriage, have no authority from ancient records,
has often been noticed. The re-marriage of widows
is not a subject on which unwritten usage can be expected to throw much light, for the Brahminical law
has generally prevailed in respect of personal family
relations, but the unwritten law of property, which
largely differs from the written law, undoubtedly
gives colour to the notion that the extraordinary
harshness of the Hindoo text-writer to widows is of
sacerdotal origin. A custom, of which there are
many traces in the ancient law of the Aryan races,
but which is not by any means confined to them,
gives under various conditions the government of
the family, and, as a consequence of government,
the control of its property, to the wife after the
death of her husband, sometimes during the minority
of her male children, sometimes for her own life
upon failure of direct male descendants, sometimes
even, in this last contingency, absolutely. But the
same feeling, gradually increasing in strength, which
led them in their priestly capacity to preach to the
widow the duty of self-immolation at her husband's
funeral-pyre, appears to have made her proprietary
rights more and more distasteful to the Brahminical
text-writers; and the Hindoo jurists of all schools,

though of some more than others, have striven
hard to maintain the principle that the life of the
widow is properly a life of self-denial and humilia-
tion. Partly by calling in the distinction between
separate and undivided property, and partly by help
of the distinction between movable and immovable
property, they have greatly cut down the widow's
rights, not only reducing them for the most part
(where they arise) to a life-interest, but abridging this
interest by a variety of restrictions to little more
than a trusteeship. Here again I am assured that
any practice corresponding to this doctrine is very
rarely found in the unwritten usage, under which
not only does the widow tend to become a true pro-
prietress for life, but approaches here and there to
the condition of an absolute owner.

The preservation, during a number of centuries
which it would be vain to calculate, of this great body
of unwritten custom, differing locally in detail, but
connected by common general features, is a phenomenon which the jurist must not pass over. Before
I say anything of the conclusions at which it points,
let me tell you what is known of the agencies by
which it has been preserved. The question has by
no means been fully investigated, but many of those
best entitled to have an opinion upon it have informed me that one great instrumentality is the
perpetual discussion of customary law by the people

themselves. We are, perhaps, too apt to forget that in all stages of social development men are comparatively intelligent beings, who must have some subjects of mental interest. The natives of India, for poor and ignorant men, have more than might be expected of intellectual quickness, and the necessities of the climate and the simplicity of their habits make the calls on their time less, and their leisure greater, than would be supposed by persons acquainted only with the labourers of colder climates. Those who know most of them assert that their religious belief is kept alive not by direct teaching, but by the constant recitation in the vernacular of parts of their sacred poems, and that the rest of their thought and conversation is given to their usages. But this, doubtless, is not the whole explanation. I have been asked —and I acknowledge the force of the question—how traditions of immemorial custom could be preserved by the agricultural labourers of England, even if they had more leisure than they have? But the answer is that the social constitution of India is of the extreme ancient, that of England of the extreme modern type. I am aware that the popular impression here is that Indian society is divided, so to speak, into a number of horizontal strata, each representing a caste. This is an entire mistake. It is extremely doubtful whether the Brahminical theory of caste upon caste was ever true except of the two

· highest castes; and it is even likely that more importance has been attached to it in modern than ever
was in ancient times.   The real India contains one
priestly caste, which in a certain, though a very
limited, sense is the highest of all, and there are,
besides, some princely houses and a certain number
of tribes, village communities, and guilds, which still
in our day advance a claim, considered by many
good authorities extremely doubtful, to belong to
the second or third of the castes recognised by the ˙
Brahminical writers.   But otherwise, caste is merely
a name for trade or occupation, and the sole tangible
effect of the Brahminical theory is that it creates a
religious sanction for what is really a primitive and
natural distribution of classes.   The true view of
India is that, as a whole, it is divided into a vast
number of independent, self-acting, organised social
groups—trading, manufacturing, cultivating.   The
English agricultural labourers of whom we spoke,
are a too large, too indeterminate class, of which
the units are too loosely connected, and have too
few interests in common, to have any great power
of retaining tradition.   But the smaller organic
groups of Indian society are very differently situated.
They are constantly dwelling on traditions of a certain sort, they are so constituted that one man's
interests and impressions correct those of another,
and some of them have in their council of elders a

permanent machinery for declaring traditional usage, and solving doubtful points. Tradition, I may observe, has been the subject of so much bitter polemical controversy that a whole group of most interesting and important questions connected with it have never been approached in the proper spirit. Under what conditions it is accurate, and in respect of what class of matters is accurate, are points with which the historical jurist is intimately concerned. I do not pretend to sum up the whole of the lessons which observation of Indian society teaches on the subject, but it is assuredly the belief of men who were at once conscientious observers and had no antecedent theory to sway them, that naturally organised groups of men are obstinate conservators of traditional law, but that the accuracy of the tradition diminishes as the group becomes larger and wider.

The knowledge that this great body of traditional law existed, and that its varieties were just sufficiently great for the traditions of one group to throw light on those of another, will hereafter deeply affect the British administration of India. But I shall have to point out to you that there are signs of its being somewhat abused. There has been a tendency to leave out of sight the distinctions which render different kinds of tradition of very different value; the distinction, for example, between a mere tradition as to the rule to be followed in a given case and a tradition which has caused a rule to be followed; the distinction, as it has been put, between customs which do and customs which do not correspond to practices. If a tradition is not kept steady by corresponding practice, it may be warped by all sorts of extraneous influences. The great value now justly attached in India to traditional law has even brought about the absurdity of asking it to solve some of the most complicated problems of modern society, problems produced by the collapse of the very social system which is assumed to have in itself their secret.

I have been conducted by this discussion to a topic on which a few words may not be thrown away. Not only in connection with the preservation of customary law, but as a means of clearing the mind before addressing oneself to a considerable number of juridical questions, I must ask you to believe that the very small place filled by our own English law in our thoughts and conversation is a phenomenon absolutely confined to these islands. A very simple experiment, a very few questions asked after crossing the Channel, will convince you that Frenchmen, Swiss, and Germans of a very humble order have a fair practical knowledge of the law which regulates their everyday life. We in Great Britain and Ireland are altogether singular in our tacit conviction that law belongs as much to the class of exclusively professional subjects as the practice of anatomy. Ours is, in fact, under limitations which it is not necessary now to specify, a body of traditional customary law; no law is better known by those who live under it in a certain stage of social progress, none is known so little by those who are in another stage. As social activity multiplies the questions requiring judicial solution, the method of solving them which a system of customary law is forced to follow is of such a nature as to add enormously to its bulk. Such a system in the end beats all but the experts; and we, accordingly, have turned our laws over to experts, to attorneys and solicitors, to barristers above them, and to judges in the last resort. There is but one remedy for this—the reduction of the law to continuous writing and its inclusion within aptly-framed general propositions. The facilitation of this process is the practical end of scientific jurisprudence.

As in the lectures which follow I shall not often appeal to what are ordinarily recognised as the fountains of Hindoo law, it was necessary for me to explain that the materials for the conclusions which I shall state—unwritten usages, probably older and purer than the Brahminical written law—are now having their authority acknowledged even by the Indian Courts, once the jealous conservators of the

integrity of the sacerdotal system.   These materials are partly to be found in that large and
miscellaneous official literature which I described as
having grown out of the labours of the functionaries
who adjust the share of the profits of cultivation
claimed by the British Government as supreme landlord; but much which is essential to a clear under-
standing can only be at present collected from the
oral conversation of experienced observers who have
passed their maturity in administrative office.   The
inferences suggested by the written and oral testimony would perhaps have had interest for few except
those who had passed, or intended to pass, a life in
Indian office; but their unexpected and (if I may
speak of the impression on myself) their most start-
ling coincidence with the writers who have recently
applied themselves to the study of early Teutonic
agricultural customs, gives them a wholly new value
and importance.   It would seem that light is pouring
from many quarters at once on some of the darkest
passages in the history of law and of society.   To
those who knew how strong a presumption already
existed that individual property came into existence
after a slow process of change, by which it disengaged
itself from collective holdings by families or larger
assemblages, the evidence of a primitive village system
in the Teutonic and Scandinavian countries had very
great interest; this interest largely increased when

England, long supposed to have had since the Norman Conquest an exceptional system of property in land, was shown to exhibit almost as many traces of joint-ownership and common cultivation as the countries of the North of the Continent; but our interest culminates, I think, when we find that these primitive European tenures and this primitive European tillage constitute the actual working system of the Indian village communities, and that they determine the whole course of Anglo-Indian administration

LECTURE III.

THE WESTERN VILLAGE COMMUNITY.

-

CONTENTS.

LECTURE III.

THE WESTERN VILLAGE COMMUNITY.

I HAVE AFFIRMED the fact to be established as well as any fact of the kind can be, that there exist in India several—and it may even be said, many—considerable bodies of customary law, sufficiently alike to raise a strong presumption that they either had a common origin or sprang from a common social necessity, but sufficiently unlike to show that each of them must have followed its own course of development. There exists a series of writings which pretend to be a statement of these customs, but this series proves to include a part only of the whole body of usage; it probably embodied from the first only one set of customary rules, and its form shows clearly that it must have had a separate and very distinct history of its own. Few assertions respecting lapse of time and the past can safely be made of anything Indian; but there can be no reasonable doubt that all this customary law is of very great antiquity. I need scarcely point out to you that such facts as these have a

F

bearing on more than one historical problem. If, for example, I am asked whether it is possible that, when the Roman empire had been overrun by the Northern races, the Roman law could be preserved by mere oral transmission in countries in which no breviaries of that law were published by the invading chiefs to keep it alive, I can only say that observation of India shows such preservation to be abstractedly possible ; and shows it moreover to be possible in the face of written records of a legal or legislative character which contain no reference to the unwritten and orally transmitted rules. But I should at the same time have to point out that nothing in India tends to prove that law may be orally handed down from one generation to another of men who form an indeterminate class, or that it can be preserved by any agency than that of organised, self-acting, social groups. I should further have to observe that, unless there have been habits and practices corresponding to the traditional rules, those rules may be suspected of having undergone considerable modification or depravation.

I pass, however, to matters which have a closer interest for the jurist, and which are, therefore, discussed with more propriety in this department of study. So long as that remarkable analysis of legal conceptions effected by Bentham and Austin is not very widely known in this country (and I see no signs

of its being known on the Continent at all), it is
perhaps premature to complain of certain errors into
which it is apt to lead us on points of historical jurisprudence. If, then, I employ the Indian legal phenomena to illustrate these errors, I must preface what
I have to say with the broad assertion that nobody
who has not mastered the elementary part of that
analysis can hope to have clear ideas either of law or
of jurisprudence. Some of you may be in a position to
call to mind the mode in which these English jurists
decompose the conception of a law, and the nature
and order of the derivative conceptions which they
assert to be associated with the general conception.
A law, they say, is a command of a particular kind.
It is addressed by political superiors or sovereigns to
political inferiors or subjects ; it imposes on those
subjects an obligation or *duty* and threatens a penalty
(or *sanction*) in the event of disobedience. The
power vested in particular members of the community
of drawing down the sanction on neglects or breaches
of the duty is called a Right. Now, without the most
violent forcing of language, it is impossible to apply
these terms, *command, sovereign, obligation, sanction,
right,* to the customary law under which the Indian
village communities have lived for centuries, practically knowing no other law civilly obligatory. It
would be altogether inappropriate to speak of a political superior commanding a particular course of action

to the villagers. The council of village elders does not
command anything, it merely declares what has
always been. Nor does it generally declare that
which it believes some higher power to have com-
manded; those most entitled to speak on the subject
deny that the natives of India necessarily require
divine or political authority as the basis of their
usages; their antiquity is by itself assumed to be a
sufficient reason for obeying them. Nor, in the
sense of the analytical jurists is there *right* or *duty* in
an Indian village community ; a person aggrieved
complains not of an individual wrong but of the disturbance of the order of the entire little society. More
than all, customary law is not enforced by a sanction.
In the almost inconceivable case of disobedience to
the award of the village council, the sole punishment,
or the sole certain punishment, would appear to be
universal disapprobation. And hence, under the
system of Bentham and Austin, the customary law of
India would have to be called morality—an inversion
of language which scarcely requires to be formally
protested against.

I shall have hereafter to tell you that in certain of
the Indian communities there are signs of one family
enjoying an hereditary pre-eminence over the others,
so that its head approaches in some degree to the
position of chief of a clan, and I shall have to explain
that this inherited authority is sometimes partially

and sometimes exclusively judicial, so that the chief becomes a sort of hereditary judge. Of communities thus
circumstanced the juristical analysis to which I have
been referring is more nearly true. So too the codified Brahminical law could be much more easily
resolved into the legal conceptions determined by
Bentham and Austin. It assumes that there is a
king to enforce the rules which it sets forth, and provides a procedure for him and his subordinates, and
penalties for them to inflict ; and moreover it becomes
true law in the juristical sense, through another
peculiarity which distinguishes it. Every offence
against this written law is also a sin ; to injure a
man's property is for instance to diminish the power
of his sons to provide properly for expiatory funeral
rites, and such an injury is naturally supposed to
entail divine punishment on its perpetrator.

We may, however, confine our attention to the
unwritten usages declared from time to time by the
council of village elders. The fact which has
greatest interest for the jurist is one which has been
established by the British dominion of India, and
which could not probably have been established
without it. It may be described in this way.
Whenever you introduce any one of the legal conceptions determined by the analysis of Bentham and
Austin, you introduce all the others by a process
which is apparently inevitable. No better proof

could be given that, though it be improper to employ these terms *sovereign, subject, command, obligation, right, sanction,* of law in certain stages of human thought, they nevertheless correspond to a stage to which law is steadily tending and which it is sure ultimately to reach.

Nothing is more certain than that the revolution of legal ideas which the English have effected in India was not effected by them intentionally. The relation of sovereign to subject, for instance, which is essential to the modern juridical conception of law, was not only not established by them, but was for long sedulously evaded. When they first committed themselves to a course of territorial aggrandisement, they adopted a number of curious fictions rather than admit that they stood to the people of India as political superior to political inferior. Nor had they the slightest design of altering the customary law of the country. They have been accused of interfering with native usages, but when the interference (which has been on the whole very small) has taken place, it has either arisen from ignorance of the existence of custom or has been forced on them, in very recent times and in the shape of express legislation, by necessities which I may be led hereafter to explain.[1] The English never therefore intended that

---

[1] I have endeavoured to redeem this promise in part by printing in an Appendix a Minute recorded in India on the subject of the over-legislation not infrequently attributed to the British Government.

the laws of the country should rest on their com-
mands, or that these laws should shift in any way
their ancient basis of immemorial usage.   One change
only they made, without much idea of its importance,
and thinking it probably the very minimum of conces-
sion to the exigencies of civilised government.   They
established Courts of Justice in every administrative
district.   Here I may observe that, though the
Brahminical written law assumes the existence of
king and judge, yet at the present moment in some
of the best governed semi-independent native States
there are no institutions corresponding to our Courts
of Justice.   Disputes of a civil nature are adjusted
by the elders of each village community, or occasionally, when they relate to land, by the functionaries
charged with the collection of the prince's revenue.
Such criminal jurisdiction as is found consists in the
interposition of the military power to punish breaches
of the peace of more than ordinary gravity.   What
must be called criminal law is administered through
the arm of the soldier.

In a former lecture I spoke of the stiffness given
to native custom through the influence of English
law and English lawyers on the highest courts of
appeal.   The changes which I am about to describe
arose from the mere establishment of local courts of
lowest jurisdiction ; and while they have effected a
revolution, it is a revolution which in the first

instance was conservative of the rigidity of native usage. The customs at once altered their character. They are generally collected from the testimony of the village elders ; but when these elders are once called upon to give their evidence, they necessarily lose their old position. They are no longer a half-judicial, half-legislative council. That which they have affirmed to be the custom is henceforward to be sought from the decisions of the Courts of Justice, or from official documents which those courts receive as evidence; such, for example, as the document which, under the name of the Record of Rights, I described to you as a detailed statement of all rights in land drawn up periodically by the functionaries employed in settling the claim of the Government to its share of the rental. Usage, once recorded upon evidence given, immediately becomes written and fixed law. Nor is it any longer obeyed as usage. It is henceforth obeyed as the law administered by a British Court, and has thus really become a command of the sovereign. The next thing is that the vague sanctions of customary law disappear. The local courts have of course power to order and guide the execution of their decrees, and thus we have at once the sanction or penalty following disobedience of the command. And, with the command and with the sanction, come the conceptions of legal right and duty. 1 am not speaking of the logical but of the practical

consequence.   If I had to state what for the moment
is the greatest change which has come over the
people of India and the change which has added most
seriously to the difficulty of governing them, I should
say it was the growth on all sides of the sense of
individual legal right; of a right not vested in the
total group but in the particular member of it
aggrieved, who has become conscious that he may
call in the arm of the State to force his neighbours to
obey the ascertained rule.   The spread of this sense
of individual right would be an unqualified advantage
if it drew with it a corresponding improvement in
moral judgment.   There would be little evil in the
British Government giving to native custom a constraining force which it never had in purely native
society, if popular opinion could be brought to approve
of the gradual amelioration of that custom.   Unfortunately for us, we have created the sense of legal
right before we have created a proportionate power
of distinguishing good from evil in the law upon
which the legal right depends.

You will see then that the English government
of India consciously introduced into India only one
of the conceptions discriminated by the juridical
analysis of a law.   This was the sanction or penalty;
in establishing Courts of Justice they of course contemplated the compulsory execution of decrees.   But
in introducing one of the terms of the series you will

observe they introduced all the others—the political
superior, the command, the legal right and the legal
duty. I have stated that the process is in itself one
conservative of native usage, and that the spirit introduced from above into the administration of the
law by English lawyers was also one which tended
to stereotype custom. You may therefore perhaps
recall with some surprise the reason which I assigned
in my first Lecture for making haste to read the
lessons which India furnishes to the juridical student.
Indian usage, with other things Indian, was, I told
you, passing away. The explanation is that you
have to allow for an influence, which I have merely
referred to as yet, in connection with the exceptional
English Courts at Calcutta, Madras, and Bombay.
Over the interior of India it has only begun to make
itself felt of late years, but its force is not yet nearly
spent. This is the influence of English law; not, I
mean, of the spirit which animates English lawyers
and which is eminently conservative, but the contagion, so to speak, of the English system of law,— the
effect which the body of rules constituting it produces by contact with native usage. Primitive customary law has a double peculiarity: it is extremely
scanty in some departments, it is extremely prodigal
of rules in others ; but the departments in which
rules are plentiful are exactly those which lose their
importance as the movements of society become

quicker and more various.   The body of persons to
whose memory the customs are committed has probably always been a quasi-legislative as well as a
quasi-judicial body, and has always added to the
stock of usage by tacitly inventing new rules to apply
to cases which are really new.   When, however, the
customary law has once been reduced to writing and
recorded by the process which I have described, it
does not supply express rules or principles in nearly
sufficient number to settle the disputes occasioned by
the increased activity of life and the multiplied wants
which result from the peace and plenty due to British
rule.   The consequence is wholesale and indiscrimi-
nate borrowing from the English law—the most
copious system of express rules known to the world.
The Judge reads English law-books ; the young
native lawyers read them, for law is the study into
which the educated youth of the country are throw-
ing themselves, and for which they may even be said
to display something very like genius.   You may
ask what authority have these borrowed rules in
India.   Technically, they have none whatever ; yet,
though they are taken (and not always correctly
taken) from a law of entirely foreign origin, they are
adopted as if they naturally commended themselves
to the reason of mankind ; and all that can be said
of the process is that it is another example of the
influence, often felt in European legal history, which

express written law invariably exercises on unwritten customary law when they are found side by side. For myself, I cannot say that I regard this transmutation of law as otherwise than lamentable. It is not a correction of native usage where it is unwholesome. It allows that usage to stand, and confirms it rather than otherwise ; but it fills up its interstices with unamalgamated masses of foreign law. And in a very few years it will destroy its interest for the historical jurist, by rendering it impossible to determine what parts of the structure are of native and what of foreign origin. Nor will the remedial process which it is absolutely necessary to apply for the credit of the British name restore the integrity of the native system. For the cure can only consist in the enactment of uniform, simple, codified law, formed for the most part upon the best European models.

It is most desirable that one great branch of native Indian usage should be thoroughly examined before it decays, inasmuch as it is through it that we are able to connect Indian customary law with what appears to have once been the customary law of the Western World. I speak of the Indian customs of agricultural tenure and of collective property in land.

For many years past there has been sufficient evidence to warrant the assertion that the oldest discoverable forms of property in land were forms of collective property, and to justify the conjecture that separate property had grown through a series (though not always an identical series) of changes, out of collective property or ownership in common. But the testimony which was furnished by the Western World had one peculiarity. The forms of collective property which had survived and were open to actual observation were believed to be found exclusively in countries peopled by the Sclavonic race. It is true that historical scholars who had made a special study of the evidence concerning ancient Teutonic holdings, as, for example, the early English holdings, might have been able to assert of them that they pointed to the same conclusions as the Sclavonic forms of village property; but the existing law of property in land, its actual distribution and the modes of enjoying it, were supposed to have been exclusively determined in Teutonic countries by their later history. It was not until Von Maurer published a series of works, in which his conclusions were very gradually developed, that the close correspondence between the early history of Teutonic property and the facts of proprietary enjoyment in the Germany of our own day was fully established; and not two years have elapsed since Nasse called attention to the plain and abundant vestiges of collective Teutonic property which are to be traced in England.

I shall not attempt to do more than give you such a summary of Von Maurer's conclusions as may suffice

to connect them with the results of official observation
and administrative enquiry in India.   You will find
a somewhat fuller compendium of them in the paper
contributed by Mr. Morier to the volume recently
published, called 'Systems of Land Tenure in Various
Countries.'   Mr. Morier is the English Chargé d'Af-
faires at Darmstadt, and he assures me that his account
of the abundant vestiges of collective property which
are to be found in the more backward parts of
Germany may easily be verified by the eye.   They
are extremely plain in some territorial maps with
which he has been good enough to supply me.

The ancient Teutonic cultivating community, as it
existed in Germany itself, appears to have been thus
organised.   It consisted of a number of families
standing in a proprietary relation to a district divided
into three parts.   These three portions were the Mark
of the Township or Village, the Common Mark or
waste, and the Arable Mark or cultivated area.   The
community inhabited the village, held the common
mark in mixed ownership, and cultivated the arable
mark in lots appropriated to the several families.

Each family in the township was governed by its
own free head or paterfamilias.   The precinct of the
family dwelling-house could be entered by nobody
but himself and those under his *patria potestas*, not
even by officers of the law, for he himself made law
within and enforced law made without.

But, while he stood under no relations controllable by others to the members of his family, he stood in a number of very intricate relations to the other heads of families. The sphere of usage or customary law was not the family, but the connection of one family with another and with the aggregate community.

Confining ourselves to proprietary relations, we find that his rights or (what is the same thing) the rights of his family over the Common Mark are controlled or modified by the rights of every other family. It is a strict ownership in common, both in theory and in practice. When cattle grazed on the common pasture, or when the householder felled wood in the common forest, an elected or hereditary officer watched to see that the common domain was equitably enjoyed.

But the proprietary relation of the householder which has most interest for us is his relation to the Arable Mark. It seems always in theory to have been originally cut out of the common mark, which indeed can only be described as the portion of the village domain not appropriated to cultivation. In this universally recognised original severance of the arable mark from the common mark we come very close upon the beginning of separate or individual property. The cultivated land of the Teutonic village community appears almost invariably to have been divided into three great fields. A rude rotation of crops was the

object of this threefold division, and it was intended
that each field should lie fallow once in three years.

The fields under tillage were not however cultivated by labour in common.   Each householder has
his own family lot in each of the three fields, and
this he tills by his own labour, and that of his sons
and his slaves.   But he cannot cultivate as he
pleases.   He must sow the same crop as the rest of
the community, and allow his lot in the uncultivated
field to lie fallow with the others.   Nothing he does
must interfere with the right of other households to
have pasture for sheep and oxen in the fallow and
among the stubbles of the fields under tillage.   The
rules regulating the modes of cultivating the various
lots seem to have been extremely careful and complicated, and thus we may say without much rashness
that the earliest law of landed property arose at the
same time when the first traces of individual property
began to show themselves, and took the form of
usages intended to produce strict uniformity of cultivation in all the lots of ground for the first time
appropriated.   That these rules should be intricate
is only what might be expected.   The simplicity
of the earliest family law is not produced by any
original tendency of mankind, but is merely the
simplicity which goes always with pure despotism.
Ancient systems of law are in one sense scanty.
The number of subjects with which they deal is

small, and, from the modern jurist's point of view,
there are great gaps in them. But the number of
minute rules which they accumulate between narrow
limits is very surprising. The most astonishing
example of this is to be found in the translation of
the Ancient Irish law now in course of publication
by the Irish Government. The skeleton of this law
is meagre enough, but the quantity of detail is vast—
so vast that I cannot but believe that much of it is
attributable to the perverted ingenuity of a class of
hereditary lawyers.

The evidence appears to me to establish that the
Arable Mark of the Teutonic village community was
occasionally shifted from one part of the general
village domain to another. It seems also to show
that the original distribution of the arable area was
always into exactly equal portions, corresponding to
the number of free families in the township. Nor
can it be seriously doubted upon the evidence that
the proprietary equality of the families composing
the group was at first still further secured by a
periodical redistribution of the several assignments.
The point is one of some importance. One stage in
the transition from collective to individual property
was reached when the part of the domain under
cultivation was allotted among the Teutonic races to
the several families of the township; another was
gained when the system of 'shifting severalties' came

to an end, and each family was confirmed for a
perpetuity in the enjoyment of its several lots of
land.   But there appears to be no country inhabited
by an Aryan race in which traces do not remain of
the ancient periodical redistribution.   It has continued to our own day in the Russian villages.
Among the Hindoo villagers there are widely extending traditions of the practice; and it was doubtless the source of certain usages, to be hereafter
described, which have survived to our day in England and Germany.

I quote from Mr. Morier's paper the following observations.   ' These two distinct aspects of the early
Teutonic freeman as a " lord " and a " commoner "
united in the same person—one when within the pale
of his homestead, the other when standing outside
that pale in the economy of the mark—should not be
lost sight of.   In them are reflected the two salient
characteristics of the Teutonic race, the spirit of
individuality, and its spirit of association; and as the
action and reaction of these two laws have determined the social and political history of the race, so
they have in an especial manner affected and determined its agricultural history.'

Those of you who are familiar with the works of
Palgrave, Kemble, and Freeman, are aware that the
most learned writers on the early English proprietary
system give an account of it not at variance in any

material point with the description of the Teutonic
mark which I have repeated from Von Maurer.   The
question, then, which at once presses on us is whether
an ancient form of property, which has left on
Germany traces so deep and durable that (again to
quote Mr. Morier) they may always be followed
on ordinary territorial maps, must be believed to have
quite died out in England, leaving no sign of itself
behind?   Unquestionably the answer furnished by
the received text-books of English real-property law
is affirmative.   They either assume, or irresistibly
suggest, that the modern law is separated from the
ancient law by some great interruption; and Nasse,
the object of whose work is to establish the survival
of the Mark in England, allows that German
enquirers had been generally under the impression
that the history of landed property in this country
was characterised by an exceptional discontinuity.
There is much in the technical theory of our real-
property law which explains these opinions; and it
is less wonderful that lawyers should have been led
to them by study of the books, than that no doubt
of their soundness should have been created by facts
with which practitioners were occasionally well
acquainted.   These facts, establishing the long con-
tinuance of joint cultivation by groups modelled on
the community of the Mark, were strongly pressed
upon the Select Committee of the House of Commons

which sat to consider the subject of inclosures in
1844 by a witness, Mr. Blamire, who was at once a
lawyer and an official unusually familiar with English
landed property in its less usual shapes.   Yet Mr.
Blamire appears ('Evidence before Select Committee
of 1844,' p. 32, q. 335) to have unreservedly adopted
the popular theory on the subject, which I believe to
be that at some period—sometimes vaguely associated
with the feudalisation of Europe, sometimes more
precisely with the Norman Conquest—the entire soil
of England was confiscated ; that the whole of each
manor became the lord's demesne; that the lord
divided certain parts of it among his free retainers,
but kept a part in his own hands to be tilled by his
villeins; that all which was not required for this
distribution was left as the lord's waste; and that all
customs which cannot be traced to feudal principles
grew up insensibly, through the subsequent tolerance
of the feudal chief.

There has been growing attention for some years
past to a part of the observable phenomena which
prove the unsoundness of the popular impression.
Many have seen that the history of agriculture, of
land-law, and of the relations of classes cannot be
thoroughly constructed until the process has been
thoroughly deciphered by which the common or
waste-land was brought under cultivation either by
the lord of the manor or by the lord of the manor

in connection with the commoners. The history of Inclosures and of Inclosure Acts is now recognised as of great importance to our general history. But corresponding study has not, or not of late, been bestowed on another set of traces left by the past. The Arable Mark has survived among us as well as the Common Mark or waste, and it the more deserves our attention in this place because its interest is not social or political but purely juridical.

The lands which represent the cultivated portion of the domain of the ancient Teutonic village communities are found more or less in all parts of England, but more abundantly in some counties than in others. They are known by various names. When the soil is arable, they are most usually called 'common,' 'commonable,' or 'open' fields, or sometimes simply 'intermixed' lands. When the lands are in grass, they are sometimes known as 'lot meadows,' sometimes as 'lammas lands,' though the last expression is occasionally used of arable soil. The 'common fields' are almost invariably divided into three long strips, separated by green baulks of turf. The several properties consist in subdivisions of these strips, sometimes exceedingly minute; and there is a great deal of evidence that one several share in each of the strips belonged originally to the same ownership, and that all the several shares in any one strip were originally equal or nearly equal, though in progress of time a

good many have been accumulated in the same hands.
The agricultural customs which prevail in these
common fields are singularly alike. Each strip bears
two crops of a different kind in turn and then lies
fallow. The better opinion seems to be that the
custom as to the succession of crops would not be
sustained at law; but the right to feed sheep or cattle
on the whole of one strip during the fallow year, or
among the stubbles of the other two strips after the
crops have been got in, or on the green baulks which
divide the three fields, is generally treated as capable
of being legally maintained. This right has in some
cases passed to the lord of the manor, but sometimes
it is vested in the body of persons who are owners of
the several shares in the common fields. The grass
lands bear even more distinct traces of primitive
usage. The several shares in the arable fields, sometimes, but very rarely, shift from one owner to
another in each successive year; but this is frequently
the rule with the meadows, which, when they are
themselves in a state of severalty, are often distributed once a year by casting lots among the persons
entitled to appropriate and enclose them, or else
change from one possessor to another in the order of
the names of persons or tenements on a roll. As a
rule the inclosures are removed after the hay-harvest;
and there are manors in which they are taken down
by the villagers on Lammas Day (that is, Old

Lammas Day) in a sort of legalised tumultuary
assembly. The group of persons entitled to use the
meadows after they have been thrown open is often
larger than the number of persons entitled to enclose them. All the householders in a parish, and
not merely the landowners, are found enjoying this
right. The same peculiarity occasionally, but much
more rarely, characterises the rights over common
arable fields; and it is a point of some interest, since
an epoch in the history of primitive groups occurs
when they cease to become capable of absorbing
strangers. The English cultivating communities may
be supposed to have admitted new-comers to a limited
enjoyment of the meadows, up to a later date than
the period at which the arable land had become the
exclusive property of the older families of the group.

The statute 24 Geo. II. c. 23, which altered the
English Calendar, recites (s. 5) the frequency of
these ancient customs and forms of property, and
provides that the periods for commencing common
enjoyment shall be reckoned by the old account of
time. They have been frequently noticed by agricultural writers, who have strongly and unanimously
condemned them. There is but one voice as to the
barbarousness of the agriculture perpetuated in the
common arable fields, and as to the quarrels and
heart-burning of which the 'shifting severalties' in
the meadow land have been the source. But both

common fields and common meadows are still plentiful on all sides of us. Speaking for myself personally, I have been greatly surprised at the number of instances of abnormal proprietary rights, necessarily implying the former existence of collective ownership and joint cultivation, which comparatively brief enquiry has brought to my notice; nor can I doubt that a hundred and fifty years ago instances of such rights could have been produced in vastly greater numbers, since Private Acts of Parliament for the inclosure of commonable fields were constantly passed in the latter part of the last and the earlier part of the present century, and since 1836 they have been extensively enclosed, agglomerated, and exchanged under the Common Fields Inclosure Act passed in that year, and under the general powers more recently vested in the Inclosure Commissioners. The breadth of land which was comparatively recently in an open, waste, or commonable condition, and which therefore bore the traces of the ancient Teutonic cultivating system, may be gathered from a passage in which Nasse sums up the statements made in a number of works by a writer, Marshall, whom I shall presently quote. 'In almost all parts of the country, in the Midland and Eastern Counties particularly, but also in the West—in Wiltshire for example—in the South, as in Surrey, in the North, as in Yorkshire, there are extensive open and common

fields. Out of 316 parishes in Northamptonshire, 89
are in this condition; more than 100 in Oxfordshire;
about 50,000 acres in Warwickshire; in Berkshire,
half the county; more than half of Wiltshire; in
Huntingdonshire, out of a total area of 240,000 acres,
130,000 were commonable meadows, commons, and
common fields.' (Ueber die Mittelalterliche Feldgemeinschaft in England,' p. 4.) The extent of some
of the fields may be inferred from the fact, stated to
me on good authority, that the pasturage on the dividing baulks of turf, which were not more than three
yards wide, was estimated in one case at eighty acres.
These footprints of the past were quite recently found
close to the capital and to the seats of both Uni-
versities. In Cambridgeshire they doubtless corresponded to the isolated patches of dry soil which were
scattered through the fens, and in the metropolitan
county of Surrey, of which the sandy and barren soil
produced much the same isolation of tillage as did the
morasses of the fen country, they occurred so close to
London as to impede the extension of its suburbs,
through the inconvenient customs which they placed
in the way of building. One of the largest of the
common fields was found in the immediate neighbourhood of Oxford; and the grassy baulks which
anciently separated the three fields are still conspicuous from the branch of the Great Northern Railway
which leads to Cambridge.

The extract from Marshall's 'Elementary and Practical Treatise on Landed Property' (London, 1804) which I am about to read to you, is in some ways very remarkable. Mr. William Marshall was a writer on agriculture who published largely between 1770 and 1820, and he has left an account of the state of cultivation in almost every English county. He had been engaged for many years in ' studying the improvement and directing the management of several large estates in England, Wales and Scotland,' and he had taken a keen interest in what he terms ' provincial practices.' The picture of the ancient state of England which follows, was formed in his mind from simple observation of the phenomena of custom, tillage, and territorial arrangement which he saw before his eyes. You will perceive that he had not the true key in his possession, and that he figured to himself the collective form of property as a sort of common farm, cultivated by the tenantry of a single landlord.

'In this place it is sufficient to premise that a very few centuries ago, nearly the whole of the lands of England lay in an open, and more or less in a commonable state. Each parish or township (at least in the more central and northern districts), comprised different descriptions of lands ; having been subjected, during successive ages, to specified modes of occupancy, under ancient and strict regulations,

which time had converted to law. These parochial
arrangements, however, varied somewhat in different
districts; but in the more central and greater part
of the kingdom, not widely; and the following statement may serve to convey a general idea of the whole
of what may be termed Common-field Townships,
throughout England.

' Under this ingenious mode of organisation, each
parish or township was considered as one common
farm ; though the tenantry were numerous.

' Round the village, in which the tenants resided,
lay a few small inclosures, or grass yards ; for rearing calves, and as baiting and nursery grounds for
other farm stock. This was the common farmstead,
or homestall, which was generally placed as near the
centre of the more culturable lands of the parish or
township as water and shelter would permit.

' Round the homestall, lay a suit of arable fields ;
including the deepest and soundest of the lower
grounds, situated out of water's way ; for raising
corn and pulse ; as well as to produce fodder and
litter for cattle and horses in the winter season.

'And, in the lowest situation, as in the water-
formed base of a rivered valley, or in swampy dips,
shooting up among the arable lands, lay an extent of
meadow grounds, or " ings " ; to afford a supply of
hay, for cows and working stock, in the winter and
spring months.

' On the outskirts of the arable lands, where the
soil is adapted to the pasturage of cattle, or on the
springy slope of hills, less adapted to cultivation, or
in the fenny bases of valleys, which were too wet, or
gravelly water-formed lands which were too dry, to
produce an annual supply of hay with sufficient certainty, one or more stinted pastures, or hams, were
laid out for milking cows, working cattle, or other
stock which required superior pasturage in summer. '

' While the bleakest, worst-soiled, and most distant
lands of the township, were left in their native wild
state; for timber and fuel; and for a common pasture,
or suit of pastures, for the more ordinary stock of
the township ; whether horses, rearing cattle, sheep,
or swine ; without any other stint, or restriction, than
what the arable and meadow lands indirectly gave ;
every joint-tenant, or occupier of the township,
having the nominal privilege of keeping as much
live-stock on these common pastures, in summer, as
the appropriated lands he occupied would maintain,
in winter.

' The appropriated lands of each township were laid
out with equal good sense and propriety.   That each
occupier might have his proportionate share of lands
of different qualities, and lying in different situations,
the arable lands, more particularly, were divided into
numerous parcels, of sizes, doubtless, according to the
size of the given township, and the number and rank
of the occupiers.

'And, that the whole might be subjected to the same plan of management, and be conducted as one common farm, the arable lands were moreover divided into compartments, or "fields," of nearly equal size, and generally three in number, to receive, in constant rotation, the triennial succession of fallow, wheat (or rye) and spring crops (as barley, oats, beans, and peas): thus adopting and promoting a system of husbandry, which, howsoever improper it is become, in these more enlightened days, was well adapted to the state of ignorance, and vassalage, of feudal times ; when each parish or township had its sole proprietor ; the occupiers being at once his tenants and his soldiers, or meaner vassals. The lands were in course liable to be more or less deserted by their occupiers, and left to the feebleness of the young, the aged, and the weaker sex. But the whole township being, in this manner, thrown into one system, the care and management of the live-stock, at least, would be easier and better than they would have been, under any other arrangement. And, at all times, the manager of the estate was better enabled to detect bad husbandry, and enforce that which was more profitable to the tenants and the estate, by having the whole spread under the eye, at once, than he would have been, had the lands been distributed in detached inclosed farmlets ; besides avoiding the expense of inclosure. And another advantage arose from this more social arrangement, in barbarous times : the tenants, by being concentrated in villages, were not only best situated to defend each other from predatory attacks ; but were called out, by their lord, with greater readiness, in cases of emergency.' (Marshall, pp. 111–113.)

The readers of the ' Pirate ' are, I dare say, aware that Sir Walter Scott had his attention strongly attracted to the so-called Udal tenures of Orkney and Shetland. The fact has more juridical interest than it once had, now that recent writers have succeeded in completely identifying the ancient Scandinavian and ancient German proprietary usages. In the diary which he wrote of his voyage with the Commissioners of Lighthouses round the coasts of Scotland, Scott observes: ' I cannot get a distinct account of the nature of the land-rights. The Udal proprietors have ceased to exist, yet proper feudal tenures seem ill understood. Districts of ground are in many instances understood to belong to townships or communities, possessing what may be arable by patches and what is moor as a commonty *pro indiviso.* But then individuals of such a township often take it upon them to grant feus of particular parts of the property thus possessed *pro indiviso.* The town of Lerwick is built upon a part of the commonty of Sound; the proprietors of the houses having feu-rights from different heritors of that township, but why

from one rather than other . . . . seems altogether
uncertain' (Lockhart's 'Life of Scott,' iii. p. 145).
That these tenures survived till lately in the northern
islands has been long known, but there has been a
general impression that the strict and consistent
feudalism of Scotland had effaced the traces of older
Teutonic usage in the Lowlands. Yet a Return
recently presented to Parliament suggests that a re-
examination of Scottish agricultural customs might
be usefully undertaken. 'There are,' it is stated,
'within the bounds of the royalty of the burgh of
Lauder 105 separate portions of land called Burgess Acres. These vary in extent from one and a
half acre to three and a half acres. To each such
acre there is a separate progress of writs, and these
" Acres " are the private and absolute property of
individuals. . . . No one has hitherto been admitted a
burgess of the burgh who has not been an owner of
one of these Burgess Acres. The lands of the burgh
consist of . . . . Lauder Common, extending to about
1,700 acres, which has, from all time of which there is
any record, been possessed thus. A portion of it has
been set off periodically, say once in five or seven
years, to be broken up and ploughed during that time,
and at the end of that time fixed has been laid down
in grass, and grazed along with the other lands :
when another portion of the common was, in the same
way, broken up and ploughed, and again laid down in

grass. The portion of the common so broken up and
ploughed at a time has, of recent years, been about
130 acres in extent. An allotment of this portion of
the common has been given to the owner of each of
the 105 burgess acres, whether he happened to be a
burgess or not, one allotment for each acre. The
portion laid off for cultivation is, in the first place,
cut into the number of allotments required, and the
share of each person is decided by lot. The conditions attached to the taking of hill parts have been,
compliance with a system of cultivation prescribed by
the town council, and payment of a small assessment,
generally just sufficient to reimburse the burgh for
expenses laid out in making roads, drains, &c., to
enhance the value of the land for cultivation. These
allotments have been called " Hill parts," and the
average worth of each is 1*l.* per annum. The whole
of the remainder of the common has been used for
grazing purposes, and has been occupied as follows:
Each burgess resident within the bounds of the burgh
has grazed on the common two cows, or an equivalent,
and a certain number of sheep—at present, and for
some years, fifteen; and each widow of a burgess,
resident in the burgh, has grazed on the common one
cow, or an equivalent, and a certain number of sheep
—at present, and for many years, twelve' (' Return
of Boroughs or Cities in the United Kingdom, possessing Common Land,' Appendix I., House of
Commons, August 10, 1870).

It may be doubted whether a more perfect example of the primitive cultivating community is extant in England or Germany. As compared with the English instances, its form is extremely archaic. The arable mark, cultivated under rules prescribed by the town council, shifts periodically from one part of the domain to another, and the assignment of parcels within the cultivated area is by lot. It is interesting too to observe that the right to land for purposes of tillage is inseparably connected with the ownership of certain plots of land within the township. A similar connection between the shares in the common field and certain ancient tenements in a village is sometimes found in England and has been formally established at law. (See the bitter complaints of Marshall, 'Rural Economy of Yorkshire,' i. 55.) On the other hand, a group of persons more loosely defined has the right to pasture on the part of the common in grass, and this peculiarity occurs also in England. I am informed that most of the Scottish burghs have recently sold their 'commonties;' but it is to be hoped that all traces of the ancient customs of enjoyment have not been quite obliterated.

Upon the evidence collected by Nasse, supplied by the works of Marshall, and furnished by the witnesses examined before the Select Committee of 1844, and upon such as I have myself been able to gather, the vestiges of the Teutonic village community which

H

remained before the inclosures of the last century and the present may be thus compendiously described : The arable part of the domain was indicated (1) by simple intermixed fields, *i.e.* fields of nearly equal size mingled together and belonging to an extraordinary number of owners, so that, according to Mr. Blamire's statement, in one parish containing 2,831 acres there were (in 1844) 2,315 pieces of open land which included 2,327 acres, giving an average size of one acre (Evidence, Select Committee, p. 17, q. 185) ; (2) by fields of nearly equal size arranged in three long strips and subject to various customs of tillage, the most universal being the fallow observed by each of the strips in successive years ; (3) by ' shifting severalties' of arable land, which were not, however, of frequent occurrence ; (4) by the existence of certain rights of pasture over the green baulks which prevented their removal.

The portion of the domain kept in grass was represented : (1) by ' shifting severalties ' of meadow land, which were very frequent, the modes of successive allotment being also very various ; (2) by the removal of inclosures after hay-harvest ; (3) by the exercise, on the part of a community generally larger than the number of persons entitled to enclose, of a right to pasture sheep and cattle on the meadowland during the period when the hay was not maturing for harvest.

The rights known to exist over Commons constitute much too large a subject to be treated of here. But two relics of the ancient collective cultivation may be specially mentioned. The supervision of the communal officer who watched over the equitable enjoyment of the pastures has become the custom of ' stint of common,' by which the number of the beasts which the commoner might turn out on the waste is limited and regulated. There is also a good deal of evidence that some commons, now entirely waste, bear the traces of ancient tillage. The most probable explanation is that in these cases the whole of the arable mark had been removed from one part of the domain to another, and that the traces of cultivation show the place of common fields anciently deserted.

LECTURE IV.

THE EASTERN VILLAGE COMMUNITY.

CONTENTS.

LECTURE IV.

THE EASTERN VILLAGE COMMUNITY.

I PROPOSE in this Lecture to describe summarily and remark upon the Indian forms of property and tenure corresponding to the ancient modes of holding and cultivating land in Europe which I discussed at some length last week. It does not appear to me a hazardous proposition that the Indian and the ancient European systems of enjoyment and tillage by men grouped in village communities are in all essential particulars identical. There are differences of detail between them, and I think you will find the discussion of these differences and of their apparent causes not uninteresting nor barren of instruction to the student of jurisprudence.

No Indian phenomenon has been more carefully examined, and by men more thoroughly in earnest, than the Village Community. For many years past the discovery and recognition of its existence have ranked among the greatest achievements of Anglo-Indian administration. But the Village Community did not emerge into clear light very early in the history of our conquest and government. Although this peculiar group is referred to in Manu, the English found little to guide them to its great importance in the Brahminical codified law of the Hindoos which they first examined. Perhaps in the large space assigned in that law to joint-property and partitions they might have found a hint of the truth, if the great province in which they were first called upon to practise administration on a large scale, Lower Bengal or Bengal Proper, had not happened to be the exact part of India in which, from causes not yet fully determined, the village system had fallen into great decay. The assumption which the English first made was one which they inherited from their Mahometan predecessors. It was, that all the soil belonged in absolute property to the sovereign, and that all private property in land existed by his sufferance. The Mahometan theory and the corresponding Mahometan practice had put out of sight the ancient view of the sovereign's rights, which, though it assigned to him a far larger share of the produce of the land than any western ruler has ever claimed, yet in nowise denied the existence of private property in land. The English began to act in perfect good faith on the ideas which they found universally prevailing among the functionaries whom they had taken over from the Mahometan semi-independent viceroys de-throned by their arms. Their earliest experiments,

tried in the belief that the soil was theirs and that
any land-law would be of their exclusive creation, have
now passed into proverbs of maladroit management.
The most famous of them was the settlement of
Lower Bengal by Lord Cornwallis. It was an attempt to create a landed-proprietary like that of this
country. The policy of conferring estates in fee
simple on the natural aristocracy of certain parts of
India (and I mean by a 'natural aristocracy' an
aristocracy formed under purely native conditions of
society by what amounts to the sternest process of
natural selection) has had many fervent advocates
among Indian functionaries, and has very lately been
carried out on a considerable scale in the newly-
conquered province of Oudh. But the great proprietors established by Lord Cornwallis were undoubtedly, with few exceptions, the tax-gatherers of
the former Mahometan viceroy. The recoil from what
was soon recognised as a mistake, brought a system
into fashion which had been tried on a small scale
at an earlier date, and which was in fact the reverse
of Lord Cornwallis's experiment. In the southern
provinces of the peninsula, the English Government
began to recognise nothing between itself and the
immediate cultivators of the soil; and from them it
took directly its share of the produce. The effect
was to create a peasant-proprietary. This system, of
which the chief seat was the province of Madras, has, in

my opinion, been somewhat unjustly decried. Now that
it has been modified in some details, and that some
mistakes first committed have been corrected, there
is no more prosperous population in India than that
which has been placed under it; but undoubtedly it
is not the ancient system of the country. It was not
till English conquest was extending far to the north-
west, and till warlike populations were subjugated
whose tastes and peculiarities it was urgently necessary to study, that the true proprietary unit of India
was discovered. It has ever since been most carefully
and continuously observed. There have been many
vehement and even violent disputes about some of
its characteristics; but these disputes will always, I
think, be found to arise, or at least to derive their
point, from an attempt to make it fit in with some
theory of English origin. There is no substantial
difference of opinion about its great features. I
regret exceedingly that I cannot refer you to any
book in which there is a clear or compendious account
of it. Perhaps the best and most intelligible is that
given by a distinguished Indian functionary, Mr.
George Campbell, in that same volume on 'Systems of
Land Tenure' to which I referred you for Mr. Morier's
summary of Von Maurer's conclusions. But the description is necessarily much too brief for a subject of
such extent, and full information must be obtained from
the extensive literature of Revenue and Settlement

which I spoke of some time since as having had its materials collected by quasi-judicial agencies. But the student who attempts to consult it should be warned that much of the elementary knowledge which has to be acquired before its value and interest can be completely understood is only at present to be gathered from the oral statements of experienced Indian functionaries. In the account of the Indian cultivating group which follows you will understand that I confine myself to fundamental points, and further that I am attempting to describe a typical form to which the village communities appear to me upon the evidence I have seen to approximate, rather than a model to which all existing groups called by the name can be exactly fitted.

If very general language were employed, the description of the Teutonic or Scandinavian village communities might actually serve as a description of the same institution in India. There is the arable mark, divided into separate lots but cultivated according to minute customary rules binding on all. Wherever the climate admits of the finer grass crops, there are the reserved meadows, lying generally on the verge of the arable mark. There is the waste or common land, out of which the arable mark has been cut, enjoyed as pasture by all the community *pro indiviso*. There is the village, consisting of habitations each ruled by a despotic pater-familias. And

there is constantly a council of government to determine disputes as to custom. But there are some
characteristics of the institution of which no traces,
or very faint traces, remain in Europe, though they
probably once existed, and there are some differences
between the European and Indian examples. Identity in the main being assumed, a good deal of
instruction may be obtained from these distinctions
of detail.

First as to the arable mark, or cultivated portion of
the village domain. Here you will naturally expect
the resemblances to be general rather than specific.
The official publications on Indian Settlement law
contain evidence that in some parts of the country
the division into three common fields is to be found;
but I do not attach any importance to the fact, which
is probably quite accidental. The conditions of
agriculture in a tropical country are so widely
different from those which can at any period be
supposed to have determined cultivation in Northern
and Central Europe as to forbid us to look for any
resemblances in India, at once widely extended and
exact, to the Teutonic three-field system. Indeed,
as the great agent of production in a tropical country
is water, very great dissimilarities in modes of
cultivation are produced within India itself by
relative proximity to running streams and relative
exposure to the periodical rain-fall. The true

analogy between the existing Indian and the ancient European systems of tillage must be sought in the minute but multifarious rules governing the proceedings of the cultivators ; rules which in both cases have the same object—to reconcile a common plan and order of cultivation on the part of the whole brotherhood with the holding of distinct lots in the arable land by separate families. The common life of the group or community has been so far broken up as to admit of private property in cultivated land, but not so far as to allow departure from a joint system of cultivating that land. There have been functionaries serving the British Government of India who have had the opportunity of actually observing the mode in which rules of this kind grow up. Wherever the great canals of irrigation which it has constructed pass through provinces in which the system of village communities survives in any completeness, the Government does not undertake—or perhaps I should rather say it has not hitherto undertaken—the detailed distribution of water to the peasants inhabiting the village. It bargains with them to take a certain quantity of water in return for a certain addition to the revenue assessed upon them, and leaves them, when the water has once been conducted to the arable mark, to divide it between themselves as they please. A number of minute rules for regu-

lating each man's share of the water and mode of
using it are then imposed on the village, by the
council of elders, by the elective or hereditary functionary who sometimes takes its place, or by the
person who represents the community in its contracts with Government for payment of land-rent.
I have been told, however, by some of those who
have observed the formation of these rules, that
they do not purport to emanate from the personal
authority of their author or authors ; nor do they
assume to be dictated by a sense of equity ; there is
always, I am assured, a sort of fiction, under which
some customs as to the distribution of water are
supposed to have existed from all antiquity, although
in fact no artificial supply had been even so much as
thought of.   It is further stated that, though it is
extremely common among English functionaries to
speak of the distribution of water as regulated by the
agreement of the villagers, yet no such idea really
enters the mind of the community or of its represen-
tatives as that there can be or ought to be an express
or implied contract among the cultivators respecting
their several shares.   And it is added that, rather
than have a contract or agreement, it would appear
to them a much more natural and reasonable arrangement that the distribution should be determined by
casting lots.   Authority, Custom, or Chance are in
fact the great sources of law in primitive communi-

ties as we know them, not Contract. Not that in the minds of men who are at this stage of thought the acknowledged sources of law are clearly discriminated. There are many customary duties of which the most plausible account that can be given is that they were at the outset obligations of kinship, sanctioned by patriarchal authority; yet childish stories attributing their origin to mere accident are often current among the Indian villagers, or they are said to be observed in obedience to the order of some comparatively modern king. I have already said that the power of the sovereign to create custom is very generally recognised in India; and it might even be said that such ideas of the obligatory force of agreement as exist are nowadays greatly mixed up with the notion of obedience to government. It is often stated that an agreement written on the stamped paper of the State acquires in the native view a quality which is quite independent of the legal operation of the stamp; and there is reason to believe that the practice, which prevails through whole provinces, of never performing an agreement till performance has been decreed by a Court, is to a very great extent accounted for by an impression that contracts are not completely binding till the State has directed them to be executed.

Among the non-Aryan peasantry who form a considerable proportion of the population in the still

thinly peopled territory called the Central Provinces,
the former highroad of Mahratta brigandage, there
are examples of the occasional removal of the entire
arable mark from one part of the village domain to
another, and of the periodical redistribution of lots
within the cultivated area.   But I have not obtained
information of any systematic removal, and still less
of any periodical re-partition of the cultivated lands,
when the cultivators are of Aryan origin.   But experienced Indian officials have told me that though
the practice of redistribution may be extinct, the
tradition of such a practice often remains, and the
disuse of it is sometimes complained of as a grievance.
If English influence has had anything to do with
arresting customs of re-partition, which are, no doubt,
quite alien to English administrative ideas, it is a
fresh example of destructive influence, unwillingly
and unconsciously exercised.   For the separate, un-
changeable, and irremovable family lot in the cultivated area, if it be a step forwards in the history of
property, is also the point at which the Indian village
community is breaking to pieces.   The probability,
however, is that the causes have had their operation
much hastened by the English, but have not been
created by them.   The sense of personal right growing everywhere into greater strength, and the ambi-
tion which points to wider spheres of action than can
be found within the Community, are both destructive

of the authority of its internal rules. Even more
fatal is the increasing feeling of the sacredness of
personal obligation arising out of contract. The par-
tition of inheritances and execution for debt levied
on land are destroying the communities—this is the
formula heard nowadays everywhere in India. The
brotherhood of the larger group may still cohere, but
the brethren of some one family are always wishing
to have their shares separately; and creditors who
would have feared to intrude on the village domain
now break the net of custom by stepping without
ceremony into the lot of a defaulting debtor.

I now pass to the village itself, the cluster of home-
steads inhabited by the members of the community.
The description given by Maurer of the Teutonic Mark
of the Township, as his researches have shown it to
him, might here again pass for an account, so far as
it goes, of an Indian village. The separate households,
each despotically governed by its family chief, and
never trespassed upon by the footstep of any person
of different blood, are all to be found there in practice;
although the theory of the absolute rights of heads of
families has never, from the nature of the case, been
acknowledged by the British Government. But the
Indian villages have one characteristic which could
only have been gathered from observation of a living
society. The German writers have been struck with
that complete immunity of the Teutonic homestead

I

from all external interference, which in this country
found a later expression in the long-descended
common-place that an Englishman's house is his
castle. But a characteristic which in India goes
along with this immunity, and to a great extent
explains it, is the extraordinary secrecy of family
life; a secrecy maintained, I am told, in very humble
households and under difficulties which at first sight
would seem insurmountable. There can be no question that, if the isolation of households in ancient
societies was always accompanied by this secrecy of
their interior life, much which is not quite intelligible in early legal history would be explained. It
is not, for example, easy to understand the tardiness
with which, in Roman society, the relations of Pater-
familias and Filius-familias became the subject of
moral judgment, determining the interference of the
Prætor; or, again, taking the form of public opinion,
and so ultimately issuing in legislation. But this
would be much more comprehensible if the secrets
of family life were nearly as carefully guarded as
they are at this moment, even in those parts of
India where the peculiar Mahometan jealousy, which
has sometimes been erroneously thought a universal Eastern feeling, has never yet penetrated.
So, again, it is only a conjectural explanation of the
scantiness of ancient systems of law as they appear
in the monuments in which an attempt was made
to set them formally forth, that the lawgiver

merely attempted to fill, so to speak, the interstices between the families, of which the aggrega-
tion formed the society.   To the extent to which
existing Indian society is a type of a primitive society,
there is no doubt that any attempt of the public lawgiver to intrude on the domain reserved to the legislative and judicial power of the pater-familias causes
the extremest scandal and disgust.   Of all branches of
law, criminal law is that which one would suppose to
excite least resentment by trespassing on the forbidden limits.   Yet, while many ignorant statements
are constantly made about the rash disturbance of
native Indian ideas by British law and administration,
there is really reason to believe that a grievance most
genuinely felt is the impartiality of that admirable
Penal Code which was not the least achievement of
Lord Macaulay's genius, and which is undoubtedly
destined to serve some day as a model for the criminal law of England.   I have had described to me a
collection of street-songs, sung in the streets of the
city which is commonly supposed to be most impa-
tient of British rule by persons who never so much as
dreamed of having their words repeated to an Englishman.   They were not altogether friendly to the
foreign rulers of the country, but it may be broadly
laid down that they complained of nothing which
might naturally have been expected to be the theme
of complaint.   And, without exception, they declared

that life in India had become intolerable since the
English criminal laws had begun to treat women
and children as if they were men.

I read to you from Mr. Morier's compendium of
Von Maurer's results, a passage pointedly contrasting the independence of the Teutonic freeman in
his homestead and its appurtenances with his complete subjection to customary rule when he cultivated
the arable mark, or pastured his sheep and cattle in
the common mark. I trust there is no presumption
in my saying that in some of the most learned writers
on the Mark, there seems to me too great a tendency
to speak of the relations of the free chiefs of Teutonic
households to one another as determined by what, for
want of a more appropriate term, must be called spon-
taneous legislation. It is no doubt very difficult, in
observing an Indian village community, to get rid of
the impression that the council of elders, which is the
only Indian counterpart of the collective assembly of
Teutonic villagers, occasionally legislates; and, if very
strict language be employed, legislation is the only
term properly expressing the invention of customary
rules to meet cases which are really new. Yet, if I
may trust the statements of several eminent Indian
authorities, it is always the fact or the fiction that
this council merely declares customary law. And
indeed, while it is quite true of India that the head
of the family is supposed to be chief of the household,

the families within the village or township would seem to be bound together through their representative heads by just as intricate a body of customary rules as they are in respect of those parts of the village domain which answer to the Teutonic common mark and arable mark. The truth is, that nothing can be more complex than the customs of an Indian village, though in a sense they are only binding on chiefs of families. The examination of these customs, which have for their object to secure a self-acting organisation not only for the community as a whole, but for the various trades and callings which fractions of it pursue, does not fall within the scope of the present Lectures, but it is a subject full of interest. I observe that recent writers are dissatisfied with the historical theory which attributes the municipal institutions of mediæval Europe to an exclusively Roman origin, and that they are seeking to take into account the usages inherited from the conquerors of the Empire. From this point of view, the customary rules securing the interdependence and mutual responsibility of the members of an Indian village community, or of the various subordinate groups which it may be shown to include, and the modes of speech in use among them, which are said to fluctuate between language implying an hereditary brotherhood and language implying a voluntary association, appear to be worthy of careful examination. There is reason

to believe that some European cities were originally
nothing more than the township-mark of a Teutonic village community which has subsequently
grown to greatness. It is quite certain that this was
the origin of the large majority of the towns which
you see marked on the map of India.   The village, in
becoming more populous from some cause or other,
has got separated from its cultivated or common domain ; or the domain has been swallowed up in it ; or a
number of different villages have been founded close
together on what was perhaps at one time unprofitable waste land, but which has become exceptionally
valuable through advantages of situation.   This last
was the origin of the great Anglo-Indian city of Calcutta, which is really a collection of villages of very
modern foundation.   Here, however, it may be
proper that I should state that the very greatest
Indian cities had a beginning of another kind.
Doubtless most of the Indian towns grew out of villages, or were originally clusters of villages, but the
most famous of all grew out of camps.   The Mogul
Emperors and the Kings of the more powerful Hindoo
dynasties differed from all known sovereigns of the
Western world, not only in the singular indefiniteness
of the boundaries of their dominions and in the perpetual belligerency which was its consequence, but in
the vast onerousness of their claims on the industry
of their subjects.   From the people of a country of

which the wealth was almost exclusively agricultural,
they took so large a share of the produce as to leave
nothing practically to the cultivating groups except
the bare means of tillage and subsistence.   Nearly all
the movable capital of the empire or kingdom was
at once swept away to its temporary centre, which
became the exclusive seat of skilled manufacture and
decorative art.   Every man who claimed to belong to
the higher class of artificers took his loom or his
tools and followed in the train of the King.   This
diversion of the forms of industry which depend on
movable wealth to the seat of the court had its first
result in the splendour of Oriental capitals.   But at
the same time it made it easier to change their site,
regarded as they continued to be in the light of the
encampment of the sovereign for the time being.
Great deserted cities, often in close proximity to one
another, are among the most striking and at first
sight the most inexplicable of Indian spectacles.
Indian cities were not, however, always destroyed by
the caprice of the monarch who deserted them to
found another capital.   Some peculiar manufacture
had sometimes so firmly established itself as to
survive the desertion, and these manufacturing towns
sometimes threw out colonies.   Capitals, ex-capitals
retaining some special art or manufacture, the
colonies of such capitals or ex-capitals, villages grown
to exceptional greatness, and a certain number of

towns which have sprung up round the temples built
on sites of extraordinary sacredness, would go far to
complete the list of Indian cities.

The Waste or common land of the Village Community has still to be considered. One point of
difference between the view taken of it in the East
and that which seems at all times to have been taken
in Europe, deserves to be specially noted. The
members of the Teutonic community appear to have
valued the village waste chiefly as pasture for their
cattle, and possibly may have found it so profitable
for this purpose as to have deliberately refrained from
increasing that cultivated portion of it which had been
turned into the arable mark. These rights of pasture
vested in the commoners are those, I need scarcely
tell you, which have descended but little modified to
our own day in our own country; and it is only the
modern improvements in the methods of agriculture
which have disturbed the balance between pasture
and tillage, and have thus tended to multiply Inclosure
Acts. But the vast bulk of the natives of India are
a grain and not a flesh-eating people. Cattle are
mostly regarded by them as auxiliary to tillage. The
view therefore generally taken (as I am told) of the
common-land by the community is that it is that part
of the village-domain which is temporarily uncultivated, but which will some time or other be cultivated
and merge in the arable mark. Doubtless it is valued

for pasture, but it is more especially valued as potentially capable of tillage.   The effect is to produce
in the community a much stronger sense of property
in common-land than at all reflects the vaguer feeling
of right which, in England at all events, characterises
the commoners.   In the later days of the East India
Company, when all its acts and omissions were very
bitterly criticised, and amid the general re-opening of
Indian questions after the military insurrection of
1857, much stress was laid on the great amount of
waste land which official returns showed to exist in
India, and it was more than hinted that better
government would bring these wastes under cultivation,
possibly under cotton cultivation, and even plant them
with English colonists.   The answer of experienced
Indian functionaries was that there was no waste land
at all in India.   If you except certain territories
which stand to India Proper much as the tracts of
land at the base of the Rocky Mountains stand to the
United States—as, for example, the Indo-Chinese
province of Assam—the reply is substantially correct.
The so-called waste lands are part of the domain of
the various communities which the villagers, theoretically, are only wanting opportunity to bring under
cultivation.   Yet this controversy elicited an admission which is of some historical interest.   It did appear
that, though the native Indian Government had for
the most part left the village communities entirely to

themselves on condition of their paying the revenue assessed upon them, they nevertheless sometimes claimed
(though in a vague and occasional way) some exceptional authority over the wastes ; and, acting on
this precedent, the British Government, at the various
settlements of Land Revenue, has not seldom interfered to reduce excessive wastes and to re-apportion
uncultivated land among the various communities of
a district.   In connection with this claim and exercise
of right you will call to mind the power vested in the
early English Kings to make grants of waste to individuals in severalty, first with and afterwards without
the consent of the Witan ; and we shall see that the
much more extensive rights acquired by the lord over
the waste than over any other portion of the village-
domain, constitute a point of capital importance in the
process known as the feudalisation of Europe.

India has nothing answering to the assembly of
adult males which is so remarkable a feature of the
ancient Teutonic groups, except the Council of Village
Elders.   It is not universally found.   Villages frequently occur in which the affairs of the community
are managed, its customs interpreted, and the disputes
of its members decided by a single Headman, whose
office is sometimes admittedly hereditary but is sometimes described as elective ; the choice being generally,
however, in the last case confined in practice to the
members of one particular family, with a strong pre-

ference for the eldest male of the kindred, if he be not
specially disqualified.   But I have good authority for
saying that, in those parts of India in which the
village community is most perfect and in which
there are the clearest signs of an original proprietary equality between all the families composing the
group, the authority exercised elsewhere by the Headman is lodged with the Village Council.   It is always
viewed as a representative body, and not as a body
possessing inherent authority, and, whatever be its
real number, it always bears a name which recalls its
ancient constitution of Five persons.

I shall have hereafter to explain that, though there
are strong general resemblances between the Indian
village communities wherever they are found in anything like completeness, they prove on close inspection
to be not simple but composite bodies, including a
number of classes with very various rights and claims.
One singular proof of this variety of interests, and at
the same time of the essentially representative character of the village council, is constantly furnished, I am
told, by a peculiar difficulty of the Anglo-Indian
functionary when engaged in 'settling' a province
in which the native condition of society has been but
little broken up.   The village council, if too numerous,
is sure to be unmanageable; but there is great pressure
from all sections of the community to be represented
in it, and it is practically hard to keep its numbers

down.   The evidence of the cultivators as to custom
does not point, I am told, to any uniform mode of
representation ; but there appears to be a general
admission that the members of the council should
be elderly men.   No example of village or of
district government recalling the Teutonic assembly
of free adult males has been brought to my notice.
While I do not affect to give any complete explanation of this, it may be proper to remember that,
though no country was so perpetually scourged with
war as India before the establishment of the Pax
Britannica, the people of India were never a military
people.   Nothing is told of them resembling that
arming of an entire society which was the earliest, as
it is the latest, phase of Teutonic history.   No rule
can be laid down of so vast a population without exceptions.   The Mahratta brigands when they first rose
against the Mahometans were a Hindoo Hill-tribe
armed to a man ; and before the province of Oudh
was annexed, extreme oppression had given an
universally military character to a naturally peaceful
population.   But, for the most part, the Indian village
communities have always submitted without resistance
to oppression by monarchs surrounded by mercenary
armies.   The causes, therefore, which in primitive
societies give importance to young men in the village
assembly were wanting.   The soldiers of the community had gone abroad for mercenary service, and

nothing was required of the council but experience and civil wisdom.

There is yet another feature of the Indian cultivating groups which connects them with primitive Western communities of the same kind. I have several times spoken of them as organised and self-acting. They, in fact, include a nearly complete establishment of occupations and trades for enabling them to continue their collective life without assistance from any person or body external to them. Besides the Headman or Council exercising quasi-judicial, quasi-legislative, power, they contain a village police, now recognised and paid in certain provinces by the British Government. They include several families of hereditary traders ; the Blacksmith, the Harness-maker, the Shoemaker. The Brahmin is also found for the performance of ceremonies, and even the Dancing-Girl for attendance at festivities. There is invariably a Village-Accountant, 'an important personage among an unlettered population, so important, indeed, and so conspicuous that, according to reports current in India, the earliest English functionaries engaged in settlements of land were occasionally led by their assumption that there must be a single proprietor somewhere, to mistake the Accountant for the owner of the village, and to record him as such in the official register. But the person practising any one

of these hereditary employments is really a servant
of the community as well as one of its component
members. He is sometimes paid by an allowance in
grain, more generally by the allotment to his family
of a piece of cultivated land in hereditary possession.
Whatever else he may demand for the wares he
produces, is limited by a customary standard of
price, very rarely departed from. It is the assignment of a definite lot in the cultivated area to
particular trades, which allows us to suspect that the
early Teutonic groups were similarly self-sufficing.
There are several English parishes in which certain
pieces of land in the common field have from time
immemorial been known by the name of a particular
trade; and there is often a popular belief that nobody,
not following the trade, can legally be owner of the
lot associated with it. And it is possible that we
here have a key to the plentifulness and persistence
of certain names of trades as surnames among us.

It is a remarkable fact that certain callings, extremely respectable and lucrative, do not appear in
India to constitute those who follow them members of the village community. Eminent officials
have assured me that, so far as their experience extends, the Grain-dealer is never a hereditary trader
incorporated with the village group, nor is he a
member of the municipality in towns which have
grown out of one or more villages. The trades thus

remaining outside the organic group are those which bring their goods from distant markets; and I shall try to show the significance of this fact hereafter.

There are in Central and Southern India certain villages to which a class of persons is hereditarily attached in such a manner as to show most unmistakeably that they form no part of the natural and organic aggregate to which the bulk of the villagers belong. These persons are looked upon as essentially impure; they never enter the village, or only enter reserved portions of it; and their touch is avoided as contaminating. It is difficult to read or listen to the accounts given of them without having the mind carried to those singular races or classes which, in certain European countries, were supposed almost to our own day to transmit from father to son the taint of a mysterious uncleanness. Yet these Indian 'outsiders,' as they have been called (by Sir H. B. Frere in 'The Church and the Age,' p. 357), to avoid using the word 'outcast,' which has a different meaning, bear extremely plain marks of their origin. Though they are not included in the village, they are an appendage solidly connected with it; they have definite village duties, one of which is the settlement of boundaries, on which their authority is allowed to be conclusive. They evidently represent a population of alien blood, whose lands have been occupied by the colonists or invaders forming

the community.   Everybody who has used his eyes
in India will be on his guard against certain ex-
travagances of the modern theory of Race, and will
be slow to believe that identity of language and
identity of religion necessarily imply identity of eth-
nical origin.   The wonderful differences of external
aspect which are readily perceived between natives
of Indian provinces speaking the same language, and
the great deviation from what is regarded as the
Aryan type of form and feature observable among
populations whose speech is a near derivative from
Sanscrit, have their most reasonable explanation in
the power of absorption which the village group
may from many indications be inferred to have
possessed in the earlier stages of development.   But
the faculty of taking in strangers from without is
one which it loses in time, and there were always
probably some materials too obstinately and obtru-
sively foreign to be completely absorbed.   Under
this last head, the ' outsiders ' of the Southern villages
apparently fall.

LECTURE V.

THE PROCESS OF FEUDALISATION.

CONTENTS.

LECTURE V.

THE PROCESS OF FEUDALISATION.

THE student of legal antiquities who has once con-
vinced himself that the soil of the greatest part of
Europe was formerly owned and tilled by proprietary
groups, of substantially the same character and composition as those which are still found in the only
parts of Asia which are open to sustained and careful observation, has his interest immediately drawn
to what, in truth, is the great problem of legal history.
This is the question of the process by which the primitive mode of enjoyment was converted into the
agrarian system, out of which immediately grew the
land-law prevailing in all Western Continental Europe
before the first French Revolution, and from which
is demonstrably descended our own existing real-
property law. For this newer system no name has
come into general use except Feudalism, a word which
has the defect of calling attention to one set only of
its characteristic incidents. We cannot reasonably
doubt that one partial explanation of its origin is, so
far as it goes, correct. It arose from or was greatly

influenced by the Benefices, grants of Roman provincial land by the chieftains of the tribes which overran the Roman Empire; such grants being conferred on their associates upon certain conditions, of which the commonest was military service. There is also tolerably universal agreement that somewhere in Roman law (though *where*, all are not agreed) are to be found the rules which determined the nature of these beneficiary holdings. This may be called the theory of the official origin of feudalism, the enjoyment of land being coupled with the discharge of certain definite duties; and there are some who complete the theory by asserting that among the Teutonic races, at all events, there was an ineradicable tendency in all offices to become hereditary, and that thus the Benefices, which at first were held for life, became at last descendible from father to son.

There is no question, as I said, that this account is more than probable, and that the Benefices either began or hastened the changes which led ultimately to feudalism. Yet I think that nobody whose mind has dwelt on the explanation, has brought himself to regard it as complete. It does not tell us how the Benefices came to have so extraordinary a historical fortune. It does not account for the early, if partial, feudalisation of countries like Germany and England, where the cultivated soil was in the hands of free and fully organised communities, and was not, like the

land of Italy or Gaul, at the disposal of a conquering
king—where the royal or national grants which re-
sembled the Benefices were probably made out of
waste land—and where the influence of Roman law
was feebly felt or not at all.

The feudalisation of any one country in Europe
must be conceived as a process including a long series
of political, administrative, and judicial changes; and
there is some difficulty in confining our discussion of
it to changes in the condition of property which belong more properly to this department of study. But
I think we may limit our consideration of the subject
by looking at it in this way. If we begin with
modern English real-property law, and, by the help
of its records and of the statutes affecting it, trace its
history backwards, we come upon a period at which
the soil of England was occupied and tilled by separate proprietary societies. Each of these societies is,
or bears the marks of having been, a compact and
organically complete assemblage of men, occupying a
definite area of land. Thus far it resembles the old
cultivating communities, but it differs from them in
being held together by a variety of subordinate relations to a feudal chief, single or corporate, the Lord.
I will call the new group the Manorial group, and
though my words must not be taken as strictly
correct, I will say that a group of tenants, autocratically organised and governed, has succeeded a

group of households of which the organisation and
government were democratic. The new group, as
known to our law, is often in a state of dissolution,
but, where it is perfect, it consists of a number of
persons holding land of the Lord by free tenures,
and of a number of persons holding land of the Lord
by tenures capable of being shown to have been, in
their origin, servile—the authority of the Lord being
exercised over both classes, although in different ways,
through the agency of a peculiar tribunal, the Court
Baron. The lands held by the first description of
tenants are technically known as the Tenemental
lands; those held by the second class constitute the
Lord's Domain. Both kinds of land are essential to
the completeness of the Manorial group. If there
are not Tenemental lands to supply a certain minimum number of free tenants to attend the Court
Baron, and, according to the legal theory, to sit with
the lord as its judges, the Court Baron can no longer
in strictness be held; if it be continued under such
circumstances, as it often was in practice, it can only
be upheld as a Customary Manorial Court, sitting for
the assessment and receipt of customary dues from
the tenants of the Domain. On the other hand, if
there be no Domain, or if it be parted with, the
authority of the Lord over the free tenants is no longer
Manorial; it becomes a Seignory in gross, or mere
Lordship.

Since much of the public waste land of our country is known to have passed by national or royal grant to individuals or corporations, who, in all probability, brought it extensively under cultivation from the first by servile labour, it cannot be supposed that each of the new Manorial groups takes the place of a Village group which at some time or other consisted of free allodial proprietors.   Still, we may accept the belief of the best authorities that over a great part of England there has been a true succession of one group to the other.   Comparing, then, the two, let us ask what are the specific changes which have taken place?   The first, and far the most important of all, is that, in England as everywhere in Western Europe, the waste or common-land of the community has become the lord's waste.   It is still ancillary to the Tenemental lands; the free tenants of the lord, whom we may provisionally take to represent the freemen of the village community, retain all their ascertained rights of pasture and gathering firewood, and in some cases similar rights have been acquired by other classes; but, subject to all ascertained rights, the waste belongs, actually or potentially, to the lord's domain.   The lord's 'right of approvement,' affirmed by the Statute of Merton, and extended and confirmed by subsequent statutes, permits him to enclose and appropriate so much of the waste as is not wanted to satisfy other existing rights; nor can it be doubted

that he largely exercises this right, reclaiming part
of the waste for himself by his personal dependants
and adding it to whatever share may have belonged
to him from the first in the cultivated land of
the community, and colonising other portions of it
with settlements of his villeins who are on their
way to become copyholders. The legal theory has
altogether departed from the primitive view; the waste
is now the lord's waste; the commoners are for the
most part assumed to have acquired their rights by
sufferance of the lord, and there is a visible tendency
in courts and text-writers to speak of the lord's rights,
not only as superior to those of the commoners, but
as being in fact of greater antiquity.

When we pass from the waste to the grass lands
which were intermediate between the common land
and the cultivated area, we find many varieties in
the degree of authority acquired by the lord. The
customs of manors differ greatly on the point. Sometimes, the lord encloses for his own benefit from
Candlemas to Midsummer or Lammas, and the
common right belongs during the rest of the year to
a class of burgesses, or to the householders of a
village, or to the persons inhabiting certain ancient
tenements. Sometimes, the lord only regulates the
inclosure, and determines the time of setting up and
removing the fences. Sometimes, other persons en-

close, and the lord has the grass when the several
enjoyment comes to an end. Sometimes, his right
of pasture extends to the baulks of turf which separate the common arable fields; and probably there is
no manorial right which in later times has been more
bitterly resented than this, since it is practically fatal
to the cultivation of green crops in the arable soil.

Leaving the meadows and turning to the lands
under regular tillage, we cannot doubt that the free
holders of the Tenemental lands correspond in the
main to the free heads of households composing the
old village community. The assumption has often
been made, and it appears to be borne out by the
facts which can be established as to the common
fields still open or comparatively lately enclosed.
The tenure of a certain number of these fields is freehold; they are parcelled out, or may be shown to have
been in the last century parcelled out, among many
different owners; they are nearly always distributed
into three strips, and some of them are even at this
hour cultivated according to methods of tillage which
are stamped by their very rudeness as coming down
from a remote antiquity. They appear to be the
lands of a class which has never ceased to be free,
and they are divided and cultivated exactly as the
arable mark of a Teutonic township can be inferred,
by a large induction, to have been divided and tilled.

But, on the other hand, many large tracts of intermixed land are still, or were till their recent enfran-
chisement, copyhold of particular manors, and some
of them are held by the intermediate tenure, known
as customary freehold, which is confined by the legal
theory to lands which once formed part of the King's
Domain.   I have not been able to ascertain the proportion of common lands held by these base tenures
to freehold lands of the same kind, but there is no
doubt that much commonable or intermixed land is
found, which is not freehold.   Since the descent of
copyhold and customary freehold tenures from the
holdings of servile classes appears to be well established, the frequent occurrence of intermixed lands
of this nature seems to bear out the inference suggested by Sir H. Ellis's enumeration of the conditions
of men referred to in Domesday Book, that, during
the long process of feudalisation, some of the free
villagers sank to the status, almost certainly not a
uniform status, which was implied in villenage.   (See
also Mr. Freeman's remark, ' Hist. Norm. Conq.' i. 97.)
But evidence, supplied from quarters so wide apart as
British India and the English settlements in North
America, leads me to think that, at a time when a
system of customary tillage widely prevailed, assemblages of people planted on waste land would be likely
to copy the system literally; and I conjecture that
parts of the great wastes undoubtedly reclaimed by

the exercise of the right afterwards called the lord's 'right of approvement' were settled by servile colonies modelled on the ancient Teutonic township.

The bond which kept the Manorial group together was evidently the Manorial Court, presided over by the lord or his representative. Under the name of Manorial Court three courts are usually included, which legal theory keeps apart, the Court Leet, the Court Baron, and the Customary Court of the Manor. I think there cannot be reasonable doubt of the legitimate descent of all three from the assembly of the Township. Besides the wide criminal and civil jurisdiction which belonged to them, and which, though it has been partly abolished, has chiefly lost its importance through insensible decay, they long continued in the exercise of administrative or regulative powers which are scarcely distinguishable from legislation. Other vestiges of powers exerted by the collective body of free owners at a time when the conceptions of legislative and judicial authority had not yet been separated, remained in the functions of the Leet Jury; in the right asserted for the free tenants of sitting as Judges in the Court Baron; and in the election of various petty officers. It is true that, as regards one of these Courts, the legal theory of its character is to a certain extent inconsistent with the pedigree I have claimed for it. The lawyers have always contended that the Court Leet only existed through the King's

grant, express or implied; and in pursuance of the
same doctrine they have laid down that, whereas the
lord might himself sit in the Court Baron, he must
have a person of competent legal learning to represent him in the Court Leet.   But this only proves
that the Court Leet, which was entrusted with the
examination of the Frankpledge, had more public
importance than the other Manorial Courts, and was
therefore more distinctly brought under the assumption which had been gradually forming itself, that
royal authority is the fountain of all justice.   Even
in the last extremity of decline, the Manorial Courts
have not wholly ceased to be regarded as the tie
which connects the common interests of a definite
group of persons engaged in the cultivation of the
soil.   Marshall ('Rural Economy of Yorkshire,' i. 27)
mentions the remarkable fact that these Courts were
sometimes kept up at the beginning of the century
by the voluntary consent of the neighbourhood in
certain districts where, from the disappearance of the
servile tenures which had enabled the Customary
Courts to be continued, the right to hold them had
been forfeited.   The manorial group still sufficiently
cohered for it to be felt that some common authority
was required to regulate such matters as the repair of
minor roads, the cleansing of rivulets, the ascertain-
ment of the sufficiency of ring-fences, the assessment
of the damages of impounded cattle, the removal of
nuisances, and the stocking of commons.

On the whole, the comparison of the Village Group with the English group which I have called Manorial rather than Feudal, suggests the following general observations. Wherever that collective ownership of land which was a universal phenomenon in primitive societies has dissolved, or gone far to dissolve, into individual property, the individual rights thus formed have been but slightly affected by the process of feudalisation. If there are reasons for thinking that some free village societies fell during the process into the predial condition of villenage—whatever that condition may really have implied—a compensating process began at some unknown date, under which the base tenant made a steady approach to the level of the freeholder. Even rights which savoured of the collective stage of property were maintained comparatively intact, provided that they were ascertained: such as rights of pasture on the waste and rights of several or of common enjoyment (as the case might be) in the grass land. The encroachments of the lord were in proportion to the want of certainty in the rights of the community. Into the grass land he intruded more than into the arable land; into the waste much more than into either. The conclusion suggested to my mind is that, in succeeding to the legislative power of the old community, he was enabled to appropriate to himself such of its rights as were not immediately valuable, and which, in the event of their becoming valuable, required legislative adjustment to settle the mode of enjoying them. Let me add that the general truth of my description of the character of the change which somehow took place, is perhaps rendered antecedently more probable by the comparison of a mature, but non-feudal, body of jurisprudence, like the Roman law, with any deeply feudalised legal system. You will remember the class of enjoyable objects which the Roman lawyers call *res nullius, res publici usûs, res omnium* or *universorum;* these it reserves to the entire community, or confers on the first taker. But, under feudalised law, nearly all these objects which are capable of several enjoyment belong to the lord of the manor, or to the king. Even Prize of War, the most significant of the class, belongs theoretically to the sovereign in the first instance. By a very singular anomaly, which has had important practical results, Game is not strictly private property under English law; but the doctrine on the subject is traceable to the later influence of the Roman law.

There must be a considerable element of conjecture in any account which may be given of a series of changes which took place for the most part in remote antiquity, and which probably were far from uniform either in character or in rate of advance. It happens, however, that the vestiges of the earlier stages of the process of feudalisation are more discernible in Germany than elsewhere, both in docu-

mentary records and on the face of the land; owing
in part no doubt to the comparatively feeble action
of that superior and central authority which has
obliterated or obscured so much in our own country.
A whole school of writers, among whom Von Maurer
has the first place, has employed itself in restoring
and interpreting these traces of the Past. How did
the Manor rise out of the Mark?—this is their way
of stating the problem. What were the causes of
indigenous growth which, independently of grants of
land by royal or national authority, were leading to
a suzerainty or superiority of one cultivating community over another, or of one family over the rest
of the families composing the village community?
The great cause in the view of these writers was the
exceeding quarrelsomeness of these little societies,
and the consequent frequency of intertribal war.
One community conquers another, and the spoil of war
is generally the common mark or waste of the worsted
community. Either the conquerors appropriate and
colonise part of the waste so taken, or they take the
whole domain and restore it to be held in dependence
on the victor-society. The change from one of these
systems to another occurred, you will remember, in
Roman history, and constitutes an epoch in the development of the Roman Law of Property. The effect
of the first system on the Teutonic communities was
inequality of property; since the common land appro-

priated and occupied does not seem to have been
equally divided, but a certain preference was given to
the members of the successful community who had
most effectually contributed to the victory.   Under
the second system, when its land was restored to
the conquered society, the superiority over it which
remained to the victor, bore the strongest analogy to
a suzerainty or lordship.   Such a suzerainty was not,
however, exclusively created by success in war.
Sometimes a community possessed of common land
exceptionally extensive or exceptionally fertile would
send colonies of families to parts of it.   Each of these
new communities would receive a new arable mark,
but such of the land as remained unappropriated
would still be the common land of all the townships.
At the head of this sort of confederacy there would,
however, be the original mother-community from
which the colonists proceeded, and there seems no
doubt that in such a state of things she claimed a superiority or suzerainty over all the younger townships.

But, even if we had the fullest evidence of the
growth of suzerainties in this inchoate shape, we
should still have advanced a very little way in trac-
ing the transmutation of the village system into the
manorial system, if it were not for another phenomenon to which Landau has more particularly called
attention.   The Teutonic communities, though their
organisation (if modern language must be employed)

can only be described as democratic, appear nevertheless to have generally had an abiding tradition that
in some one family, or in some families, the blood
which ran in the veins of all the freemen was purest;
probably because the direct descent of such family or
families from a common ancestor was remembered or
believed in. From the members of these families,
the leader for a military expedition would as a rule
be chosen; but as in this stage of thought the different
varieties of power were not distinguished from one
another, the power acquired by the chieftain would
be a combination of political, military, and judicial
power. The choice of the leader would in great
emergencies be a true election, but on less serious
occasions would tend to become an acquiescence in
the direction of the eldest male agnate of the family
which had the primacy of the township. Similarly
the power which had at first been more military than
anything else, would in more peaceful times tend
rather to assume a political and judicial form. The
leader thus taken from the privileged family would
have the largest share of the lands appropriated from
conquered village-societies; and there is ground for
supposing that he was sometimes rewarded by an
exceptionally large share of the common land belonging to the society which he had headed. Everything in
fact which disturbed the peaceful order of the village
system led to the aggrandisement of the leading

L

family and of its chief.   Among the privileges which
he obtained was one of which the importance did not
show itself till much later.   He became powerful
enough in his own township to sever his own plot of
land from the rest, and, if he thought fit, to enclose
it; and thus to break up or enfeeble that system of
common cultivation under rules of obligatory custom
which depended mainly on the concurrence of all the
villagers.

There were therefore, in the cultivating communities of the German and Scandinavian races, causes
at work which were leading to inequality of property
in land.   There were causes at work which were
leading to the establishment of superiorities or suzerainties of one township over another.   There were
causes at work which tended to place the benefits of
an unequal proprietary system and the enjoyment of
these suzerainties in the hands of particular families,
and consequently of their chiefs for the time being.
Here you have all the elements of the system we are
compelled to call feudal.   But the system in its
ultimate development was the result of a double set
of influences.   One set, which I have been describing,
were of primitive growth.   Another showed themselves when powerful Teutonic monarchies began to
be formed, and consisted in grants of national waste
land or of the soil of conquered provinces.   Doubtless
some of the grantees were chiefs of families already

risen to power under indigenous Teutonic conditions; but in any case a Beneficiary would be a chieftain of a peculiarly powerful class. The cultivators of his land would either be persons settled on it by himself, or they would be vanquished provincials who had no rights which he did not choose to recognise or concede. It is not, therefore, surprising that there should have been a completer constitution of feudalism in the countries which at the time of conquest were filled with Romanised populations. The mould would be Teutonic, but the materials would be unusually plastic, and here would more especially come into play the influence of Roman law, giving precision to relations which under purely Teutonic social conditions may have been in a high degree vague and indefinite. It is well known that this systematic feudalism reacted upon the more purely Teutonic societies and gave an impulse to changes which were elsewhere proceeding at a slower pace.

I have very briefly summarised the results of a very long and laborious enquiry, and only so far as is necessary for my immediate purpose. Merely remarking that I can see little or nothing in the conclusions of these eminent German writers which is out of harmony with the account given by English scholars of the parallel phenomena of change manifested in England before the Conquest, I proceed to ask, following the scheme of these Lectures, whether

the experience of Englishmen in India throws any
light or has any bearing upon the questions which
have been occupying us?   It is not too much to say
that the phenomena observed in the East, and those
established in the West by historical research, illustrate one another at every point.   In India these dry
bones live.   Not only, as I have told you, is the
Village Community the basis of British administration
in those provinces in which the art of government
has to be practised with skill and caution, but a
number of controversies turning on the mode of
transition from the village system to what I have
called the manorial system are as earnestly, and sometimes even as violently, debated by our countrymen
in the East as are the great aspects of politics among
ourselves.   All Indian disputes take, I should explain,
a historical or antiquarian shape.   The assumption
universally made is that the country must be governed
in harmony with the established usages of the natives,
and each administrative school has therefore to justify
its opinions by showing that the principles to which
it adheres are found in some sense or other to underlie
the known customary law of India.   The extrava-
gance of partisanship which here shows itself in
unqualified assertion of the universal applicability
of general propositions has its Indian counterpart in
unqualified assertion of the universal existence of
particular customs.   The Indian controversy is, how-

ever, a controversy about facts which, though they are more complex than the disputants suppose, are nevertheless much simpler than the material of English political controversy; and the results are therefore proportionately more instructive to the by-stander who has entire sympathy with neither party.

Let us suppose a province annexed for the first time to the British Indian Empire. The first civil act of the new government is always to effect a settlement of the land revenue; that is, to determine the amount of that relatively large share of the produce of the soil, or of its value, which is demanded by the sovereign in all Oriental States, and out of which all the main expenses of government are defrayed. Among the many questions upon which a decision must be had, the one of most practical importance is, ' Who shall be settled with?'—with whom shall the settlement be made? What persons, what bodies, what groups, shall be held responsible to the British Government for its land revenue? What practically has to be determined is the unit of society for agrarian purposes; and you find that, in determining it, you determine everything, and give its character finally to the entire political and social constitution of the province. You are at once compelled to confer on the selected class powers co-extensive with its duties to the sovereign. Not that the assumption is ever made that new proprietary powers are conferred on it,

but what are supposed to be its rights in relation to all
other classes are defined; and in the vague and floating
order of primitive societies, the mere definition of a
right immensely increases its strength. As a matter
of fact, it is found that all agrarian rights, whether
superior or subordinate to those of the person held
responsible to Government, have a steady tendency to
decay. I will not ask you to remember the technical
names of the various classes of persons ' settled with '
in different parts of India—Zemindars, Talukdars,
Lumberdars—names which doubtless sound uncouth,
and which, in fact, have not an identical meaning
throughout the country—but I dwell on the fact that
the various interests in the soil which these names
symbolise are seen to grow at the expense of all others.
Do you, on entering on the settlement of a new
province, find that a peasant proprietary has been
displaced by an oligarchy of vigorous usurpers, and
do you think it expedient to take the government
dues from the once oppressed yeomen? The result is
the immediate decline, and consequently bitter dis-
content, of the class above them, who find themselves
sinking to the footing of mere annuitants on the land.
Such was the land settlement of Oudh, which was
shattered to pieces by the Sepoy mutiny of 1857, and
which greatly affected its course. Do you, reversing
this policy, arrange that the superior holder shall be
answerable to Government? You find that you have

created a landed aristocracy which has no parallel in wealth or power except the proprietors of English soil. Of this nature is the more modern settlement of the province of Oudh, only recently consummated ; and such will ultimately be the position of the Talukdars, or Barons, among whom its soil has been divided. Do you adopt a policy different from either of those which I have indicated and make your arrangements with the representative of the village community? You find that you have arrested a process of change which was steadily proceeding. You have given to this peculiar proprietary group a vitality which it was losing, and a stiffness to the relations of the various classes composing it which they never had before.

It would be a mere conceit to try to establish any close analogy between the Teutonic Kings and the British government of India. Yet, so much as this is true and instructive. The only owner of the soil of India with whom the English Government has any relations, is, in its eyes, a mere functionary. It chooses him where it pleases, and exacts from him services, chiefly pecuniary, but to a certain small extent personal. It is found, however, that when an official appointed by a powerful government acts upon the loose constitution of a primitive society he crushes down all other classes and exalts that to which he himself belongs. But for recent legislation this process would have gone to any length in India, and would have assuredly affected many other provinces than those which were its immediate theatre. It may, at least, be said that by observing it we gain a clearer conception of the effect of beneficiary gifts on the general tenure of land, and that we better understand the enormous power acquired by the chieftains who rendered immediate services to the Teutonic kings.

The English in India appear to have started with the assumption of the Mahometans that the sovereign might lawfully select anybody he pleased as the collector of his revenue; but they soon accepted the principle that the class to be 'settled with' was the class best entitled to be regarded as having rights of property in the soil. At a later date they discovered that, even when this class was determined, they had to decide what it was that proprietary rights over Indian land implied, and what powers they carried with them. No questions fuller of inherent difficulties were ever proposed for solution. As regards the first of them, the functionaries administering India might, with some eminent exceptions, but still not unfairly, be distributed into two great schools— the partisans of the theory that the soil belongs to the peasantry either as individuals or as organised in groups; and the partisans of the theory that ownership of the soil ought to be, and but for British influence would be, everywhere in India vested in some sort of native aristocracy. As regards the second

question, the Indian officials are much more exactly
divided into those who contend that the highest right
of property acknowledged to exist over the soil
carries with it the same powers which attach to an
English owner in fee-simple of the present day, and
into those who are of opinion that, if these powers are
to square with native idea and custom, they must be
more or less limited and controlled. The controversies on these two points are the most vehemently debated of Indian disputes ; and none ever presented
greater difficulties to the person who tries to form an
opinion on their merits, not from his own knowledge
but upon the evidence supplied to him by others.
He finds men of the utmost experience, of trained
power of observation, and of the most unquestionable
good faith, stating precisely opposite conclusions with
precisely equal positiveness.   But if he avail himself
of the advantage given him by the parallel facts of
European tenure, he will, perhaps, venture to have an
opinion, and to think that in these, as in many other
fierce disputes, both sides are right and both sides
are wrong.

There is no doubt that the first point at issue was
much obscured, and attention diverted to irrelevant
matter, by the unlucky experiment tried at the end
of the last century by Lord Cornwallis. A province,
like Bengal Proper, where the village system had
fallen to pieces of itself, was the proper field for the
creation of a peasant proprietary ; but Lord Cornwallis

turned it into a country of great estates, and was compelled to take his landlords from the tax-gatherers of his worthless predecessors. The political valuelessness of the proprietary thus created, its failure to obtain any wholesome influence over the peasantry, and its oppression of all inferior holders, led not only to distrust of the economical principles implied in its establishment, but to a sort of reluctance to believe in the existence of any naturally privileged class in the provinces subsequently acquired and examined. The most distinguished public servants of that day have left much on record which implies an opinion that no ownership of Indian land was discoverable, except that of the village communities, subject to the dominion of the State.

But in fact it appears that, of all the landmarks on the line of movement traced by German and English scholars from the Village group to the Manorial group, there is not one which may not be met with in India, saving always the extreme points at either end. I have not had described to me any village community under the unmodified collective government of the heads of households, but there are those who think they find the vestiges of the original constitution in a sort of democratic spirit and habit of free criticism which prevail even when the government has passed to an hereditary officer. If any thoroughly authenticated example could be produced

of a community exercising absolute liberty of choice
in electing its Headman, it would point still more
significantly to an unmodified original equality; but
the preference alleged to be invariably shown to the
members of particular families appears to show that
these elections belong really to the phenomena of
hereditary succession. It is not, however, disputed
that villages are found in great numbers in which
the government is lodged with a council, neither
claiming to be nor regarded as being anything more
than a representation of the entire cultivating body.
The instances, however, in which the authority has
passed to some particular family or families are
extremely numerous. Sometimes the office of Headman belongs absolutely to the head of a particular
family; sometimes it belongs to him primarily, but
he may be set aside for incapacity or physical blemish;
sometimes there is a power of choosing him limited
to an election between the members of one or more
privileged households. The powers which he enjoys—
or which it perhaps should be said, he would enjoy
under native conditions of society—are also very
various. But the judicial power of mediating in
disputes and of interpreting customs appears to be
certainly vested in him, together with the duty
of keeping order; and, independently of the functions which he discharges with the consent of his
neighbours, the British Government often expressly

confides to him a certain amount of regular jurisdiction and of regular authority in matters of police.

There is no question that many of the families
whom the English have recognised as owners of
villages were privileged families enjoying the primacy
of the township ; but the widest difference of opinion
has prevailed as to the nature and origin of the rights
claimed by certain families for their chiefs over
whole tracts of country, embracing the domain of
several village communities. It has been strongly
contended on one side that these great proprietors
are nothing but the descendants of farmers of the
revenue under Native Governments ; on the other it
is asserted that in some cases at all events they were
Chieftains of Clans who were selected by preference to
represent the Royal or Imperial native government
in districts in which they had an hereditary influence.
There appears to me reasonable evidence that this
last theory is true of certain localities in India. Clan
society is also in Europe the Celtic form of the family
organisation of society; and, for myself, I have great
difficulty in conceiving the origin of customary law
otherwise than by assuming the former existence of
larger groups, under patriarchal chieftains, which at
a later date dissolved into the independent collections of families forming the cultivating communities of the Teutonic (including the Scandinavian)
races and of the Hindoos.

If it be taken for granted that the English in India

were bound to recognise rights of property somewhere, their selection of the persons in whom these
rights should vest does not seem to have been as
absurd as the adherents of one Indian school are in
the habit of hinting, if not of asserting. Claims to
some sort of superior right over land in fact existed
which corresponded to every single stage through
which the conception of proprietorship has passed
in the Western world, excepting only the later
stages. The variety of these claims was practically
infinite, and not only did not diminish, but greatly
increased, as native customs and ideas were more
accurately examined. Even when the village communities were allowed to be in some sense the proprietors of the land which they tilled, they proved on
careful inspection not to be simple groups, but highly
composite bodies, composed of several sections with
conflicting and occasionally with irreconcilable claims.
The English officials solved a problem of almost
hopeless perplexity by registering all the owners of
superior rights as landowners, their conception of
ownership being roughly taken from their own
country; but the fundamental question very soon
revived under another form in the shape of the
second issue disputed between the Indian administrative schools, which is, whether proprietorship in
India is to be taken to be the same assemblage of
powers which constitutes the modern English ownership of land in fee-simple.

It seems to me that the error of the school which asserts the existence of strong proprietary rights in India, lies much less in merely making this assertion than in assuming the existence of a perfect analogy between rights of property as understood in India and as understood in this country. The presumption is strongly against the reality of any such correspondence. The rights of property are, in the eye of the jurist, a bundle of powers, capable of being mentally contemplated apart from one another and capable of being separately enjoyed. The historical enquirer can also, whenever there are materials for a history of the past, trace the gradual growth of the conception of absolute property in land. That conception appears to me, for reasons which I shall afterwards assign, to have grown out of the ownership of the lord in that portion of his domain which he cultivated by his immediate personal dependants, and therefore to be a late and gradually matured fruit of the feudalisation of Europe. A process closely resembling feudalisation was undoubtedly once at work in India ; there are Indian phenomena answering to the phenomena of nascent absolute ownership in England and Europe; but then these Indian phenomena, instead of succeeding one another, are all found existing together at the present moment. The feudalisation of India, if so it may be called, was never in fact completed. The characteristic signs of its consummation are wanting. It may

be doubted whether in any single instance the whole
power of regulating the affairs of the village community had passed to an hereditary official when the
English entered the country ; on the other hand, in
the enormous majority of examples there are peculiarities of organisation which show conclusively that
the village-group is either unmodified or has not yet
nearly passed into the manorial group.   Even, however, were we at liberty to believe that India has been
completely feudalised, we should still be as far as
possible from being entitled to assume that the highest Indian form of ownership corresponds to the absolute ownership of the English holder in fee-simple.
It has been said that many persons talk and write as
if all the Englishmen who lived between the Norman
Conquest and the Reformation lived at exactly the
same time ; but this Indian assumption implies that
there has been no change in our conception of landed
property between the epoch at which England became completely feudal and the epoch (let us say) at
which the Corn-laws were repealed.   Yet during all
these centuries England has been legislatively and to
a great extent judicially centralised, and has been
acted on by economical influences of very great uniformity.   India, from the earliest ages till the British
entered it, was under the dominion of comparatively
powerful kings, who swept away the produce of the
labour of the village communities and carried off the

young men to serve in their wars, but did not otherwise meddle with the cultivating societies. This was
doubtless the great cause of their irregular development. Intertribal wars soon gave way to the wars
of great kings leading mercenary armies, but these
monarchs, with few and doubtful exceptions, neither
legislated nor centralised. The village communities
were left to modify themselves separately in their
own way.

This subject is one of much practical importance,
and I propose to treat of the more difficult problems
which it raises in the next Lecture; at present I will
content myself with repeating that there seems to me
the heaviest presumption against the existence in
any part of India of a form of ownership conferring
the exact rights on the proprietor which are given by
the present English ownership in fee-simple. There
are now, however, a vast number of vested rights in
the country, fully recognised by the English Government, which assume the identity of Indian and
English proprietorship, and neither justice nor policy
permits them to be disturbed. Moreover it is abstractedly possible that further observation of particular localities by accurate observers may, so far as
regards those localities, rebut the presumption of
which I have spoken, provided that the enquirer be
acquainted with the parallel phenomena which belong
to European legal history, and provided that he possess

the faculty, not very common among us, of distinguishing the rudimentary stages of legal thought from
its maturity.   The way in which, among the unlettered members of a primitive society, law and morality
run into one another ought especially to be studied.
The subordinate holder who in India states that the
superior holder has the power to do a certain act, but
that he ought not to do it, does not make an admission ; he raises a question of the utmost difficulty.

It has been usual to speak of the feudalisation of
Western Europe as if it had been an unmixed evil,
and there is but too much reason to believe that it
was accompanied in its course by a great amount of
human suffering.   But there are some facts of Indian
experience which may lead us to think that the
advantage of some of the economical and juridical
results which it produced has been underrated.   If
the process indeed had really consisted, as some of
the enthusiasts for its repetition in India appear to
suppose that it did, merely in the superposition of
the lord over the free owners of land, with power
to demand such services or dues as he pleased and
to vary his demands at pleasure, very little indeed
could be said for it.   But this picture of it is certainly untrue of our own country.   We are not at
liberty to assume that the obligations incurred by the
free owner of land who *commended* himself to a lord
were other than, within certain limits, fixed and

M

definite services; and the one distinguishing characteristic which the English feudists discover in that
free Socage tenure for which the English villagers
most probably exchanged their allodial ownership is
certainty, regularity and permanence of service.   The
great novelties which the transition from one form of
property to another produced were, the new authority
over the waste which the lord acquired (and which
was connected with the transfer to him of the half
judicial, half legislative, powers of the collective
community) and the emancipation of the lord within
his own domains from the fetters of obligatory agricultural custom.   Now Europe was then full of great
wastes, and the urgent business in hand was to reclaim
them.   Large forests were to be felled, and wide
tracts of untilled land had to be brought under
cultivation.   In England, inexorably confined within
natural boundaries, there pressed with increasing force
the necessity for adopting the methods of agriculture
which were fitted to augment the total supply of food
for a growing population.   But for this work society
organised in village communities is but little adapted.
The Indian administrators who regard the cultivating
groups with most favour, contend that they secure a
large amount of comfort and happiness for the families
included within them, that their industry is generally,
and that their skill is occasionally, meritorious.   But
their admirers certainly do not claim for them that

they readily adopt new crops and new modes of tillage, and it is often admitted that they are grudging and improvident owners of their waste land. The British Government, as I before stated, has applied a remedy to this last defect by acting on the right to curtail excessive wastes which it inherited from its predecessors; and of late years it has done its utmost to extend and improve the cultivation of one great staple, Cotton—amid difficulties which seem to be very imperfectly understood by those who suppose that in order to obtain the sowing of a new crop, or the sowing of an old crop in a new way, from a peasant in bondage to hereditary custom, it is enough to prove to him that it is very likely to be profitable. There is Indian evidence that the forms of property imitated from modern English examples have a value of their own, when reclamation has to be conducted on a large scale, or novelties in agriculture have to be introduced. The Zemindars of Lower Bengal, the landed proprietary established by Lord Cornwallis, have the worst reputation as landlords, and appear to have frequently deserved it; but the grants of land originally made to them included great uncultivated tracts, and at the time when their power over subordinate holders was least limited they brought large areas of waste land under tillage by the colonies of peasants which they planted there. The proprietorship conferred on them has also much to do with the introduction into Lower Bengal, nearly alone among Indian provinces, of new and vast agricultural industries, which, if they had been placed under timely regulation (which unfortunately they were not) would have added as much to the comfort of the people as they have added to the wealth of the country.

It appears therefore to me to be highly probable that the autocratically governed manorial group is better suited than the village group for bringing under cultivation a country in which waste lands are extensive. So also does it seem to me likely to have been at all times more tolerant of agricultural novelties. It is a serious error to suppose that the non-feudal forms of property which characterised the cultivating communities had any real resemblance to the absolute property of our own day. The land was free only in the sense of being free from feudal services, but it was enslaved to custom. An intricate net of usage bound down the allodial owner, as it now binds the Indian peasant, to a fixed routine of cultivation. It can hardly be said that in England or Germany these usages had ceased to exercise a deadening influence even within living memory, since very recent writers in both countries complain of the bad agriculture perpetuated by custom in the open common fields. The famous movement against Inclosures under the Tudor reigns was certainly in part provoked by inclosures of plots in the three common fields made with the intention of breaking the custom and extending the systematic cultivation of grasses; and it is curious to find the witnesses examined before the Select Committee of 1844 using precisely the same language which was employed by the writers who in the sixteenth century took the unpopular side, and declaring that the value and produce of the intermixed lands might be very greatly increased if the owner, instead of having one plot in each field, had three plots thrown together in one field and dealt with them as he pleased. As I said before, it seems to me a plausible conjecture that our absolute form of property is really descended from the proprietorship of the lord in the domain which— besides planting it with the settlements of 'unfree' families—he tilled, when it was close to his castle or manor-house, by his own dependants under his own eye. He was free from the agricultural customs which shackled those below him, and the services exacted from above were not of a kind to affect his management of the land which he kept in his hands. The English settlers on the New England coast did not, as I shall point out, at first adopt this form of property, but they did so very shortly, and we unquestionably owe to it such an achievement as the cultivation of the soil of North America.

If, however, a society organised in groups on the

primitive model is ineffective for Production, so also
if left to develop itself solely under primitive influences it fails to secure any considerable improvement
in Distribution.   Although it is hardly possible to
avoid speaking of the Western village groups as in
one stage democratically governed, they were really
oligarchies, as the Eastern communities always tend
to become.   These little societies had doubtless
anciently a power of absorption, when men were of
more value than land.   But this they lose in time.
There is plenty of evidence that, when Western
Europe was undergoing feudalisation, it was full of
enthralled classes; and I imagine that the authority
acquired by the feudal chief over the waste was much
more of an advantage than the contrary to these
classes, whom he planted largely there in colonies
which have probably been sometimes mistaken for
assemblages of originally free villagers.   The status
of the slave is always deplorable; the status of
the predial slave is often worse than that of the
personal or household slave ; but the lowest depth
of miserable subjection is reached when the person
enthralled to the land is at the mercy of peasants,
whether they exercise their powers singly or in
communities.

Whether the Indian village communities had
wholly lost their capacity for the absorption of
strangers when the British dominion began, is a

point on which I have heard several contradictory opinions; but it is beyond doubt that the influence of the British Government, which in this respect is nothing more than the ordinary influence of settled authority, has tended steadily to turn the communities into close corporations. The definition of rights which it has effected through its various judicial agencies—the process of law by which it punishes violations of right—above all the money value which it has given to all rights by the security which it has established from one end of India to another—have all helped to make the classes in possession of vested rights cling to them with daily increasing tenacity. To a certain small extent this indirect and unintended process of shutting the door to the acquisition of new communal rights has been counteracted by a rough rule introduced by the English, and lately engrafted on the written law, under which the cultivator of the soil who has been in possession of it for a period of years is in some parts of India protected against a few of the extreme powers which attach to ownership of the modern English type. But the rule is now in some discredit, and the sphere of its operation has of late been much curtailed. And my own opinion (which I shall state more at length in the next Lecture) is, that even if the utmost effect were given to it, it would not make up for some of the inequalities of distribution between

classes actually included in the village group which
have made their way into it through the influence of
economical ideas originating in the West. On the
whole the conclusion which I have arrived at concerning the village communities is that, during the
primitive struggle for existence they were expansive
and elastic bodies, and these properties may be perpetuated in them for any time by bad government.
But tolerably good government takes away their
absorptive power by its indirect effects, and can only
restore it by direct interposition.

It was part of my design to append to these
Lectures an epitome of the work in which Professor
Nasse has attempted to connect the actual condition
of landed property in much of England at the end of
the last century as shown in the various publications
of Marshall, with the early English forms of tenure
and cultivation as known to us through the labours
of English and German scholars. But I have aban-
doned my intention on learning that Nasse's book is
likely to be made generally accessible through an
English translation. The undertaking is one which
presents considerable difficulties. Nasse complains
of the unusual scarcity of English records bearing
on tenure and agricultural custom, but in this place
we may note another class of difficulties having
its source in those abundant technicalities of English
real-property law which are so hard to read by any-

body except the professional lawyer; and yet another in the historical theory of their land law which almost all English lawyers have adopted, and which colours all English treatises and all the decisions of English Courts—a theory which, it is not unjust to say, practically regards the manorial system as having no ascertainable antecedents, and all rights *primâ facie* inconsistent with it as having established themselves through prescription and by the sufferance of the lord. I may be allowed to say that the book in which Nasse has knotted together the two ends of the historical thread is a very extraordinary one to be written by a foreigner. Much of it deals with matter which can only be discussed appropriately in other departments of study; but I may notice in this place one set of causes, of a purely juridical nature, which, besides those assigned by Nasse, tended in later times to throw small or yeomen properties into the hands of large landowners. The popular opinion much exaggerates the extent to which this accumulation of landed properties had proceeded before the great inclosures of the last century, but still it had gone some length, and undoubtedly one cause was the influence, not at first strongly felt, of the Statute of Devises. Each landed proprietor ultimately acquired the power—within limits certainly, but very wide ones—to create a private law for his own estate. The efforts of English judges to introduce order into

this chaos made it rather worse; for the expedient
which they adopted for the purpose was to give a
forced technical meaning to the popular language of
testators.   One large and complex branch of English
law is still concerned with the rules for construing
in a technical sense the loose popular expressions
found in wills.   Every estate, willed away by a testator technically unlearned, was in danger of being
burdened with a mass of conflicting rights and interests, for the most part never contemplated by the
testator himself.   There was only one way of insuring
oneself against this consequence, and that was the
employment of an expert to make the will; but there
is reason to believe that the wholesale employment
of legal experts which is now one of the singularities
of this country is of comparatively modern date, since
it is one of the traditions of the English Bar, derived
from the last generation of lawyers, that among the
great sources of litigation were at one time wills
made by village schoolmasters.   Estates thus burdened could only be held by very rich men; as they
alone could provide and insure against the technical
traps which abounded in the private law under which
the land was held, or could render them innocuous by
continued possession ending in a prescriptive title.   It
is impossible not to see that the practice of unshackled devise tended to bring small estates into the
market as unprofitable to the holders through the

complication of interests in them, and at the same time tended to make them purchaseable by rich men only.

The simple truth is that, if a system of small or peasant holdings is to continue, the power of testators must be severely restrained in order to produce simplicity in the law of the estate. It does not at all follow that the restrictions must be those of the Code Napoleon; but restrictions there must be, and I venture to think that a not unsatisfactory solution of the problem is to be found in the law by which the Indian Government has recently sought to control the power of will-making, which the early English judges either introduced into India or invested with proportions which had never belonged to it before.

THE EARLY HISTORY OF PRICE AND RENT.

CONTENTS.

LECTURE VI.

THE EARLY HISTORY OF PRICE AND RENT.

THE VILLAGE COMMUNITIES which are still found in the
Eastern world, exhibit, at first sight, a much simpler
structure than appears on close examination.   At the
outset they seem to be associations of kinsmen, united
by the assumption (doubtless, very vaguely conceived) of a common lineage.   Sometimes the community is unconnected with any exterior body, save
by the shadowy bond of caste.   Sometimes it ac-
knowledges itself to belong to a larger group or clan.
But in all cases the community is so organised as to
be complete in itself.   The end for which it exists is
the tillage of the soil, and it contains within itself the
means of following its occupation without help from
outside.   The brotherhood, besides the cultivating
families who form the major part of the group, com-
prises families hereditarily engaged in the humble arts
which furnish the little society with articles of use
and comfort.   It includes a village watch and a
village police, and there are organised authorities for

the settlement of disputes and the maintenance of civil order.

But, when the Indian village communities are more carefully scrutinised, a more complex structure discloses itself. I told you that some dominant family occasionally claims a superiority over the whole brotherhood, and even over a number of separate villages, especially when the villagers form part of a larger aggregate, tribe or clan. But, besides this, the community itself is found, on close observation, to exhibit divisions which run through its internal framework. Sometimes men of widely different castes, or Mahometans and Hindoos, are found united in the same village group; but in such cases its artificial structure is not disguised, and the sections of the community dwell in different parts of the inhabited area. But the most interesting division of the community —though the one which creates most practical difficulty—may be described as a division into several parallel social strata. There are, first, a certain number of families who are traditionally said to be descended from the founder of the village; and I may here repeat a statement made to me that the agricultural traditions of India, differing in this from the heroic traditions which furnish a subject to the great Sanscrit poems, imply that the occupation of the rich Indian plains was a process rather of colonisation than of conquest. Below these families, descended from the originators of the colony, there are others, distributed into well ascertained groups. The brotherhood, in fact, forms a sort of hierarchy, the degrees of which are determined by the order in which the various sets of families were amalgamated with the community. The tradition is clear enough as to the succession of the groups and is probably the representation of a fact. But the length of the intervals of time between each successive amalgamation, which is also sometimes given and which is always enormous, may be safely regarded as untrustworthy; and, indeed, numbers count for nothing in the East.

The relations of these component sections to one another have furnished Eastern statesmen with the problem which, of all others, has perplexed them most. For it has been necessary to translate them into proprietary relations. The superiority of each group in the hierarchy to those below it bears undoubtedly some analogy to superiority of ownership in the land which all alike cultivate. But the question has been, What is the superiority to carry with it when translated into a higher right of property? What division is it to imply of the total produce of the village domain? What power is it to confer of dealing with the land itself? A law of tenure and tenancy had in fact to be constructed, not only outside but inside the cultivating group.

N

It is easy to see that these questions were not of
the kind on which traditions were likely to throw any
considerable light.   For traditions, as I before stated,
though tenaciously preserved by organised primitive
societies, are only thoroughly to be depended upon
when there have been acts and practices corresponding to them.   It is extremely likely that the traditional respect of each group of families within the
community for those above it did occasionally take
some concrete form, but it is in the highest degree
improbable that the various layers of the little society
were connected by anything like the systematic payment of rent.   For what is it which in primitive states
of society forces groups of men to submit to that amalgamation of strangers with the brotherhood which
seems at first forbidden by its very constitution?   It is
the urgency of the struggle for existence—a struggle
in the West probably both with man and with nature—
in the East a struggle less with savage enemies than
with nature, not indeed unkindly, but extraordinarily
capricious, and difficult to subdue from her very
exuberance.   The utmost available supply of human
labour at first merely extracts from the soil what is
sufficient for the subsistence of the cultivating group,
and thus it is the extreme value of new labour which
condones the foreign origin of the new hands which
bring it.   No doubt there comes a time when this
process ceases, when the fictions which conceal it seem

to die out, and when the village community becomes a close corporation. As soon as this point is reached there is no doubt that any new-comers would only be admitted on terms of paying money or rendering service for the use and occupation of land. But in India, at all events, another set of influences then came into play which have had the effect of making the vestiges of the payment of rent extremely faint and feeble. All Oriental sovereigns feed their courts and armies by an unusually large share of the produce of the soil which their subjects till. The Indian monarchs of whose practices we have any real knowledge took so much of the produce in the shape of land-revenue as to leave to the cultivating groups little more than the means of bare subsistence. There is no discernible difference in this respect between the Mahometan Emperors of Delhi, the Mahratta princes who were dividing the Mogul Empire between them when the English first appeared, or the still more modern Hindoo sectaries, called the Sikhs, from whom we conquered the Punjab. Such nobility as existed was supported not by rents but by assignments of the royal revenue; and the natural aristocracy of the country would have differed in little from the humbler classes but for these assignments, or for the money which stuck to their fingers as the tax-gatherers of the king. The fund out of which rent is provided

is in fact a British creation—the fruit of the peace
which the British have kept and of the moderation of
their fiscal demands.

It is sometimes said, in connection with this subject,
that the idea of property in land is realised with
extreme distinctness by the natives of India. The
assertion is true, but has not the importance which
it at first appears to possess. Between village community and village community, between total group and
total group, the notion of an exclusive right to the
domain is doubtless always present; and there are
many striking stories current respecting the tenacity
with which expelled communities preserve traditions
of their ancient seat. But to convince himself that,
as regards the interior of the group, the notion of
dependent tenures connecting one stratum with another are very imperfectly conceived, it is only necessary for an impartial person to read or listen to the
contradictory statements made by keen observers of
equal good faith. The problem of Indian Rent cannot
be doubted to be one of great intrinsic difficulty. To
see this, it need only be stated. The question is not
one as to a custom, in the true sense of the word ;
the fund out of which rent comes has not hitherto
existed or has barely existed, and hence it has not
been asserted on either side of the dispute that
rent (as distinct from the Government revenue) was
paid for the use or occupation of land before the

establishment of the British Empire, or that, if it was
paid, it bore any relation to the competition value of
cultivable soil.   Nor was it an enquiry as to a tradition, because the further you recede from the beginning of British rule the greater is your distance
from the conditions under which the exaction of
competition rent for land becomes conceivable.   The
true problem can only be stated by making an assumption contrary to the fact.   Assume a market for land
and assume the existence of the fund out of which
rent comes—what primitive ideas can be traced which
point to the distribution of the fund in any particular
way?   Such is the question.   It is on the whole, I
think, to be regretted that the British Government
allowed its servants to embark on such an enquiry.
However desirable it may be to govern the natives
of the country in harmony with their own ideas, the
effect of attempting to grapple with a problem under
such vague conditions has led to violent recoils of
opinion and practice on a matter in which settled
policy was pre-eminently counselled by justice and
prudence ; and in this case it would have been better,
I think, to abandon the historical mode of dealing
with a practical question peculiar to the Indian
government, to choose the social and economical principles on which it was intended to act, and to adhere
to them until their political unsoundness was established.   But to the student of legal history the ques-

tion is one of very considerable interest, and, however
little suited it may be for the Council chamber, it
may very excusably be handled in this place.

. When first, amid the general discredit of the experiment tried by Lord Cornwallis in Bengal Proper,
the Indian administrators of fifty years or sixty years
since began to recognise the village community as
the true proprietary unit of the country, they had
very soon to face the problem of rent. They in some
cases recognised an ownership superior to that of the
village itself ; though it is alleged by their critics that
they did not recognise it as much as they ought to
have done. Within the village community they in
all cases recognised a hierarchy of minor groups,
distinguished in some way by the difference of their
rights in the soil. Besides their observation of Indian
phenomena, which was here (as I have explained)
conducted under extraordinary difficulties, they had
nothing to guide them to a conclusion except the English forms of property in land; and they probably
accepted unreservedly from the lawyers of that day
the belief that the system actually obtaining in England was not only the ancient system of the country
but that it was semi-sacred. A further misleading
influence was the phraseology already introduced by
the Economists. Between customary rents and competition rents they did not fail to distinguish, and would
probably not have denied that, as a matter of fact,

customary rents were more common and, as a matter
of recorded history, were more ancient than competition rents.   But still, misled by an error which has of
late been very justly compared with a still more famous
delusion of the Roman lawyers, they believed competition-rents to be, in some sense or other, more
natural than customary rents, and to competition-
rents only they gave the name Rent, unqualified by
an epithet.   This peculiar and (as it seems to me) improper selection of a cardinal term is not probably of
much importance in this country; but few sufficiently
instructed persons, who have followed recent Indian
controversies, can have failed to observe that almost
all the obscurities of mental apprehension which are
implied in the use of Nature as a juridical term cluster in India round the word, Rent.   Still there was
too much around the earliest Anglo-Indian observers
which seemed inconsistent with (to say the least) the
universal occurrence in India of the English relation
between landlord and tenant-at-will for them to
assume unhesitatingly that the absolute ownership of
the soil was vested in some one class, and that the rest
of the cultivating community were simply connected
with the proprietary class by paying for the use of
the land whatever the members of that class saw fit to
demand.   They did assume that the persons who were
acknowledged to be entitled to have the highest rights
in the soil, whether within the community or without

it, bore a very close analogy to English landowners in
fee simple. They further took for granted that the
great mass of the cultivators were tenants-at-will of
the English pattern. But they gave effect to their
doubts of the correctness of these analogies by creating
between landowner and tenant-at-will an intermediate
class of protected, or, as they are called in the East,
' occupancy ' tenants. When, under the government
dispossessed by the British, any cultivator was shown
to have held his land by himself or his ancestors for
a certain space of time, he was declared to be entitled
to a qualified protection against eviction and rack-rent.
By a recent legislative enactment this principle has
been generalised, and any cultivator who even under
the British Government has been undisturbed by his
landlord for the like period is invested, in some parts of
India, with the same protection. But at first the rule,
of which the origin is uncertain, was probably intended
as a rough way of determining a class which in some
sense or other was included within the village community. The exact period of occupation selected
was twelve years; the longest time during which it
seems to have been thought safe to carry back into
native society an enquiry upon legal evidence into a
question of fact.

On this rule the most vehement of controversies
has arisen. It is strongly asserted by a school of
observation and theory which has many adherents in

the present day that close examination of village
communities does not show that mere lapse of time
conferred any rights on one section of the group as
against another. In Indian disputes, as in many
others, the advantage is at first with destructive
criticism, and, upon the evidence which I have seen,
I am on the whole disposed to think that the school
of which I am speaking is in the right. The errors
into which it has fallen appear to me to begin at a
subsequent point. Some of its adherents seem to
think that a certain correspondence being assumed to
exist between a certain Indian class and owners of
land in England, and a certain correspondence being
further assumed between another Indian class and
English tenants, the inference inevitably follows that
the correspondence must be so close as to imply all
the incidents of the English relation of landlord and
tenant-at-will. But the Indian forms of property in
land are founded on the Village Group as the proprietary unit ; the English forms are based partly on
the Manorial Group and partly on a state of things
produced by its disintegration—systems historically
so wide apart can hardly be used even to illustrate
one another. There are other adherents of the same
opinion who, conscious perhaps of the true difficulty,
attempt to get over it by asking the peasants belonging to the village community what their customs are
as to eviction, rack-rent, and the relation of landlord

and tenant. Now, if there were the faintest reason
for supposing that there ever existed in India an
open market for land and a system of competition-
rents, such an enquiry would be of great importance,
for unquestionably cultivating village groups are
highly retentive of tradition. But, eviction being
admitted to have been rarely (if ever) practised, and
it being allowed that rent was never paid for the use
of land or (if paid) was not paid on any scale which
indicated its principle, to ask a peasant whether a
given class of tenants ought or ought not to be
subject to rack-rent and eviction is to put to a very
ignorant man a question at once extremely complex,
extremely ambiguous, and only capable of being
answered (so far as it can be answered at all) after a
careful examination of the parallel phenomena of
many different ancient systems of law. The reference
to the peasantry is doubtless honestly made, but it is
an appeal to the least competent of tribunals.

The question, What vestiges remain of ancient ideas
as to the circumstances under which the highest obtainable rent should be demanded for the use of land,
is of some interest to the student of legal antiquities;
although even in this place it is not a question which
can be very confidently answered. The most distinct
ancient rule which I have discovered occurs in the
first of the official volumes containing the version of
the Ancient Laws of Ireland published by the Irish

Government. 'The three rents,' it says, 'are rack-rent, from a person of a strange tribe—a fair rent, from one of the tribe—and the stipulated rent, which is paid equally by the tribe and the strange tribe.' (Senchus Mor, p. 159.)

This very much expresses the conclusion on the subject which I have arrived at upon the less direct evidence derived from a variety of quarters. The Irish clan was apparently a group much more extensive and of much looser structure than the Eastern or Western village community; it appears even to have embraced persons who cannot be distinguished from slaves. Yet from none of these (apart from express agreement) could any rent be required but a rent fair according to received ideas, or, in other words, a customary rent. It was only when a person totally unconnected with the clan by any of those fictions explaining its miscellaneous composition which were doubtless adopted by this (as by all other) primitive groups—when such a person came asking for leave to occupy land, that the best bargain could be made with him to which he could be got to submit. 'Rack-rent' is sometimes used as a dyslogistic expression for an extreme competition-rent; but you will see that ideas associated with competition-rents in the economical sense have no relation whatever to such a transaction. In a primitive society the person who submits to extreme terms from one group is

pretty sure to be an outcast thrown on the world by
the breaking up and dispersion of some other group,
and the effect of giving him land on these terms is
not to bring him under the description of a tenant
as understood by the Economists, but to reduce him
to a condition resembling predial servitude. I need
hardly add that, in stating what seem to me the
circumstances under which a rack-rent could be demanded according to primitive ideas, I am merely
drawing an antiquarian inference, and expressing no
opinion whatever on the political expediency or otherwise of limiting the claim of a landlord to rent.

The enquiry into these primitive ideas may also
be conducted by another route, which I will follow for
a brief space on account of some curious collateral
questions which it opens. Let me begin by saying
that the remains of ancient Roman law forcibly
suggest that in ancient times transfers of the possession of land were extremely rare. The formalities
which accompanied them were of extraordinary cum-
brousness, and these formalities had to be strictly
observed not only in transactions which we should
call Conveyances, but also in the transactions which
at a later date were styled Contracts. The ancient
law further gives reason to think that the letting and
hiring of movable property for a consideration was
unknown or uncommon. The oldest Roman contracts
systematically treated of are the Real Contracts, and

to this class belongs Loan; but the loans there spoken
of are gratuitous, and the rules laid down grew
probably out of the practice of lending from house
to house the small articles of movable property in
use among a primitive people.   There is some interest in observing the plentifulness of these rules in
a system so comparatively mature as Roman law
when contrasted with their scantiness in English
jurisprudence.   The explanation seems to be that the
abundant manufacture nowadays of all articles of
personal property causes them to be much oftener
owned than lent, so that minute rules on the subject
of gratuitous loans become superfluous.

It would almost certainly be labour wasted to
search among the records of ancient law for any trace
of the ideas which we associate with competition-
rents.   But if land in primitive times was very rarely
sold or (in our sense) rented, and if movable property was very rarely hired for money, it is at least
probable that from a very early date movables were
purchased.   It does not appear to me quite an hopeless undertaking to trace the gradual development
of the notions connected with Price; and here, if at
all, we shall be able to follow the early history of
bargaining or competition.   Nor, if we can discover
any primitive ideas on the point, need we hesitate to
transfer them from the sale of movables to the competition-rent of land.   The Roman lawyers remark

of the two contracts called Emptio Venditio, or Sale
for Price, and Locatio Conductio, or Hiring for Consideration, that they are substantially the same, and
that the rules which govern one may be applied to
the other. The observation seems to me not only
true, but one which it is important to keep in mind.
You cannot indeed without forcing language speak
of the Contract of Sale in terms of the Contract of
Letting and Hiring; but the converse is easy, and
there is no incorrectness in speaking of the Letting
and Hiring of Land as a Sale for a period of time,
with the price spread over that period. I must confess I could wish that in some famous books this
simple truth had been kept in view. It has several
times occurred to me, in reading treatises on Political
Economy, that if the writer had always recollected
that a competition-rent is after all nothing but price
payable by instalments, much unnecessarily mysterious language might have been spared and some
(to say the least) doubtful theories as to the origin
of rent might have been avoided. The value of this
impression anybody can verify for himself.

What, in a primitive society, is the measure of
Price ? It can only be called Custom. Although in
the East influences destructive of the primitive notion
are actively at work, yet in the more retired villages
the artificer who plies an ancient trade still sells his
wares for the customary prices, and would always

change their quality rather than their price—a preference, I must remark, which has now and then ex-
posed the natives of India to imputations of fraud not
wholly deserved.   And in the West, even in our own
country, there are traces of the same strong feeling
that price should be determined by Custom in the
long series of royal, parliamentary, and municipal
attempts to fix prices by tariff.   Such attempts are
justly condemned as false political economy, but it is
sometimes forgotten that false political economy may
be very instructive history.

What, then, is the origin of the proposition on
which the whole of the great deductive science of
Political Economy is based? No good political econo-
mist asserts that, as matter of fact, everybody asks
for his saleable commodities the highest obtainable
price ; still less does he assert that everybody ought
to ask it.   What he lays down is that the practice of
asking it is sufficiently general to make it safe for
practical purposes to treat it as universal.   When,
however, we are discussing the ideas of very primitive
societies, it is extremely difficult to draw the line
between law, morality, and fact.   It is of the very
essence of Custom, and this indeed chiefly explains its
strength, that men do not clearly distinguish between
their actions and their duties—what they ought to do
is what they always have done, and they do it.

What, then, is the origin of the rule that a man

may ask—or, if you choose so to put it, that he does
ask—the highest available price for the wares which
he has to sell?   I think that it is in the beginning a
Rule of the Market, and that it has come to prevail
in proportion to the spread of ideas originating in
the Market.   This indeed would be a proposition of
little value, if I did not go farther.   You are well
aware that the fundamental proposition of Political
economy is often put as the rule of buying in the
cheapest market and selling in the dearest.   But
since the primitive period the character of markets
has changed almost as much as that of society itself.
In order to understand what a market originally was,
you must try to picture to yourselves a territory
occupied by village communities, self-acting and as
yet autonomous, each cultivating its arable land in
the middle of its waste, and each, I fear I must add,
at perpetual war with its neighbour.   But at several
points, points probably where the domains of two or
three villages converged, there appear to have been
spaces of what we should now call neutral ground.
These were the Markets.   They were probably the
only places at which the members of the different primitive groups met for any purpose except warfare, and
the persons who came to them were doubtless at first
persons specially empowered to exchange the produce
and manufactures of one little village community for
those of another.   Sir John Lubbock in his recent

volume on the 'Origin of Civilisation,' has some
interesting remarks on the traces which remain of
the very ancient association between Markets and
Neutrality (p. 205); nor—though I have not now
an opportunity of following up the train of thought
—can I help observing that there is an historical
connection of the utmost importance to the moderns
between the two, since the Jus Gentium of the
Roman Prætor, which was in part originally a
Market Law, is the undoubted parent of our In-
ternational Law.   But, besides the notion of neutrality, another idea was anciently associated with
markets.   This was the idea of sharp practice
and hard bargaining.   The three ideas seem all
blended in the attributes of the god Hermes or
Mercury—at once the god of boundaries, the prince
of messengers or ambassadors, and the patron of
trade, of cheating, and of thieves.

The Market was then the space of neutral
ground in which, under the ancient constitution of
society, the members of the different autonomous
proprietary groups met in safety and bought and
sold unshackled by customary rule.   Here, it seems
to me, the notion of a man's right to get the best
price for his wares took its rise, and hence it spread
over the world.   Market Law, I should here observe,
has had a great fortune in legal history.   The Jus
Gentium of the Romans, though doubtless intended

o

in part to adjust the relations of Roman citizens to a subject population, grew also in part out of commercial exigencies, and the Roman Jus Gentium was gradually sublimated into a moral theory which, among theories not laying claim to religious sanction, had no rival in the world till the ethical doctrines of Bentham made their appearance. If, however, I could venture to detain you with a discussion on technical law, I could easily prove that Market Law has long exercised and still exercises a dissolving and transforming influence over the very class of rules which are profoundly modifying the more rigid and archaic branches of jurisprudence. The Law of Personal or Movable Property tends to absorb the Law of Land or of Immovable Property, but the Law of Movable Property tends steadily to assimilate itself to the Law of the Market. The wish to establish as law that which is commercially expedient is plainly visible in the recent decisions of English courts of justice; a whole group of legal maxims having their origin in the law of the market (of which the rule of *caveat emptor* is the most significant) are growing at the expense of all others which compete with them; and there is a steady tendency in English legislation to engraft new rules, as from time to time they are developed by traders, upon the commercial law of England. Finally, the most recent of Indian disputes is whether native opinion admits of including in the Civil Code of the country the rule that a man who in good faith has purchased goods of another shall have them, though the seller had really no title to them and though the owner claim them. This is in reality an extreme rule of Market Law, and it is often described in fact as the rule of Market Overt, since it only obtains in England where that description of market exists.

Political Economists often complain of the vague moral sentiments which obstruct the complete reception of their principles. It seems to me that the half-conscious repulsions which men feel to doctrines which they do not deny might often be examined with more profit than is usually supposed. They will sometimes be found to be the reflection of an older order of ideas. Much of moral opinion is no doubt in advance of law, for it is the fruit of religious or philosophical theories having a different origin from law and not yet incorporated with it. But a good deal of it seems to me to preserve rules of conduct which, though expelled from law, linger in sentiment or practice. The repeal of the Usury Laws has made it lawful to take any rate of interest for money, yet the taking of usurious interest is not thought to be respectable, and our Courts of Equity have evidently great difficulty in bringing themselves to a complete recognition of the new principle. Bearing this example in mind, you may not think it an idle question if I ask, What is the real origin of the feeling that it is not creditable to drive a hard bargain with a near relative or a friend? It can hardly be said that there is any rule of morality to forbid it. The feeling seems to me to bear the traces of the old notion that men united in natural groups do not deal with one another on principles of trade. The only natural group in which men are now joined is the family; and the only bond of union resembling that of the family is that which men create for themselves by friendship. It is stated that there is the strongest repulsion among the natives of India to that extreme rule of Market Law which I described to you as proposed to be engrafted on the civil code. The point is doubtful on the evidence, but, considering the prevalence and vitality of organised natural groups in India, the *à priori* presumption is certainly in favour of the existence of the alleged repugnance.

All indications seem to me therefore to point to the same conclusion. Men united in those groups out of which modern society has grown do not trade together on what I may call for shortness commercial principles. The general proposition which is the basis of Political Economy, made its first approach to truth under the only circumstances which admitted of men meeting at arm's length, not as members of the same group, but as strangers. Gradually the assumption of the right to get the best price has penetrated into the interior of these groups, but it is never completely received so long as the bond of connection between man and man is assumed to be that of family or clan-connection. The rule only triumphs when the primi-tive community is in ruins. What are the causes which have generalised a Rule of the Market until it has been supposed to express an original and funda-mental tendency of human nature, it is impossible to state fully, so multifarious have they been. Every-thing which has helped to convert society into a col-lection of individuals from being an assemblage of families, has helped to add to the truth of the assertion made of human nature by the Political Economists. One cause may be assigned, after observation of the East, in the substitution of caravan or carrying trade for the frequentation of markets. When the first system grows up, the merchant, often to some extent invested with the privileges of an ambassador, carries his goods from the place of production, stores them in local entrepôts, and sells them on the principles of the Market. You will here call to mind the curious fact, stated to me on high authority, that the Grain-Dealer, though a man of great consequence and wealth, is often excluded in India from village or municipal privileges to which the small tradesmen whose busi-ness is an ancient appendage of the community are freely admitted. I am also informed that the natives of India will often pay willingly a competition price for one article, when they would think it unjust to be asked more than a customary price for another. A

man who will pay the price of the day for corn collected from all parts of India, or for cotton-cloth from
England, will complain (so I am told) if he is asked
an unaccustomed price for a shoe.

If the notion of getting the best price for movable
property has only crept to reception by insensible
steps, it is all but certain that the idea of taking the
highest obtainable rent for land is relatively of very
modern origin. The rent of land corresponds to the
price of goods, but doubtless was infinitely slower in
conforming to economical law, since the impression of
a brotherhood in the ownership of land still survived
when goods had long since become the subject of
individual property. So strong is the presumption
against the existence of competition rents in a
country peopled by village communities that it
would require the very clearest evidence to convince me that they were anywhere found under
native conditions of society, but the evidence (as I
told you) is remarkably unconvincing. I of course
admit that certain classes of people are so slightly
connected with the village community that, under
the new conditions introduced into India by the
English, their rents would probably have become
competition rents. The problem, however, presented
by these classes is not antiquarian but political. It
is identical with that terrible problem of pauperism
which began to press on English statesmen as soon

as the old English cultivating groups began distinctly
to fall to pieces.   In India the solution will be far
more difficult than it has proved here, since the
country has little mineral fuel and can have no
manufactures on a scale to occupy a large surplus
population; and emigration for the most part is
regarded as mortal sin.

The right to take the highest obtainable rent for
land is, as a matter of fact and as a matter of
morality, a right derived from a rule of the market.
Both the explanation and the justification of the
exercise of the right in England and Scotland is that
in these countries there really is a market for land.
Yet it is notorious that, in England at all events,
land is not universally rackrented.   But where is it
that the theoretical right is not exercised?   It is
substantially true that, where the manorial groups
substituted for the old village groups survive, there
are no rackrents.   What is sometimes called the
feudal feeling has much in common with the old
feeling of brotherhood which forbade hard bargains,
though like much else it has passed from the collective
community to the modern representative of its auto-
cratic chieftain.   Even in England the archaic rules
I have been describing have not yet quite lost their
authority.

Here I conclude the Lectures of the Term.   Their
chief object, as I have repeatedly stated, has been to

establish a connection between the results of Indian experience and observation and the conclusions arrived at by German and English learning. But another purpose will have been served if some of those who have attended here are induced to help in adding to our knowledge of ancient English tenures. In spite of the information collected by the Select Committee of 1844, we know far too little of Common and Commonable fields, of Lammas lands, Common meadows, and limited rights over Wastes, and generally of manorial customs. Yet forms of property, savouring of the old collective enjoyment, seem to occur so frequently that almost anybody has the opportunity of collecting facts which may have an important bearing on our enquiry. The speculative interest of the subject I need scarcely enlarge upon, but these ancient joint-holdings have a farther interest as constituting not only some of the oldest, but some of the most lasting phenomena of English history. It is a striking remark of Nasse that the English common field system bears the marks of an exotic origin. In the time of the ruder agriculture which has now given way to scientific tillage, the natural fitness of the soil of England was for grass farming, and the tendency to resort to it as the most profitable form of cultivation was apparently irresistible, and out of it grew some very serious agrarian movements. The three-field system was therefore brought by our Teutonic ancestors from some drier

region of the Continent. It is a very remarkable
fact that the earliest English emigrants to North
America—who, you know, belonged principally to
the class of yeomanry—organised themselves at first
in village-communities for purposes of cultivation.
When a town was organised, the process was that
' the General Court granted a tract of land to a company of persons. The land was first held by the
company as property in common.' (Palfrey, 'History
of New England,' ii. 13.) An American commentator
on this passage adds: ' The company of proprietors
proceeded to divide the land by assigning first house-
lots (in Marlborough from fifteen to twenty acres),
then tracts of meadow land, and in some cases
mineral land, i.e. where bog-iron ore was found.
Pasture and woodland remained in common as the
property of the company, but a law of the General
Court in 1660 provided that "hereafter no cottage
or dwelling-house be admitted to the privilege of
commonage for wood, timber, or herbage but such
as are already in being, or shall be erected with the
consent of the town." From that time the commoners appear as a kind of aristocracy, and the
commons were gradually divided up.' This is not
only a tolerably exact account of the ancient European and existing Indian village-community, but it is
also a history of its natural development, where the
causes which turn it into a manorial group are absent,
and of its ultimate dissolution.

APPENDICES.

APPENDIX I.[1]

THE first conclusion which I draw (from a Paper ' showing in each case the authority at whose suggestion the Acts of the Governor-General in Council, from No. I. of 1865, to No. XXXVIII. of 1867, were passed ') is, that next to no legislation originates with the Supreme Government of India. The only exceptions to complete inaction in this respect which are worth mentioning, occur in the case of Taxing Acts—though, as there is often much communication with the Provincial Governments on the subject of these Acts, the exception is only partial—and in that of a few Acts adapting portions of English Statute law to India. Former Indian Legislatures introduced into India certain modern English Statutes, limiting their operation to ' cases governed by English law.' The most recent English amendments of the Statutes were, however, not followed in this country until they were embodied in Indian Acts by my predecessor, Mr. Ritchie, and myself, in accordance with the general wish of the Bench and Bar of the High Courts. Examples of this sort of legislation are Acts XXVII. and XXVIII. of 1866, which only apply to ' cases governed by English law.'

The second and much the most important interference which the Paper appears to me to suggest is, that the great bulk of the legislation of the Supreme Council is

[1] Vide p. 70.

attributable to its being the Local Legislature of many
Indian Provinces. At the present moment, the Council
of the Governor-General for making Laws and Regulations
is the sole Local Legislature for the North-Western Provinces, for the Punjab, for Oudh, for the Central Provinces,
for British Burmah, for the petty Province of Coorg, and
for many small patches of territory which are scattered
among the Native States.   Moreover, it necessarily divides
the legislation of Bengal Proper, Madras, and Bombay
with the local Councils of those Provinces. For, under
the provisions of the High Court's Act of 1861, it is only
the Supreme Legislature which can alter or abridge the
jurisdiction of the High Courts, and as this jurisdiction is
very wide and far-reaching, the effect is to throw on the
Governor-General's Council no small amount of legislation
which would naturally fall on the Local Legislatures.
Occasionally, too, the convenience of having but one law
for two Provinces, of which one has a Council and the
other has none, induces the Supreme Government to legislate for both, generally at the request of both their Governments.

Now these Provinces for which the Supreme Council is
the joint or sole Legislature, exhibit very wide diversities.
Some of these differences are owing to distinctions of race,
others to differences of land-law, others to the unequal
spread of education.   Not only are the original diversities
between the various populations of India believed nowadays to be much greater than they were once thought to
be, but it may be questioned whether, for the present at
all events, they are not rather increasing than diminishing
under the influence of British Government. That influence has no doubt thrown all India more or less into
a state of ferment and progress, but the rate of progress
is very unequal and irregular.   It is growing more and
more difficult to bring the population of two or more Pro-

vinces under any one law, which goes closely home to their daily life and habits.

Not only, then, are we the Local Legislature of a great many Provinces, in the sense of being the only authority which can legislate for them on all or certain subjects, but the condition of India is more and more forcing us to act as if we were a Local Legislature, of which the powers do not extend beyond the Province for which we are legislating. The real proof, therefore, of our over-legislation would consist, not in showing that we pass between thirty and forty Acts in every year, but in demonstrating that we apply too many new laws to each or to some one of the Provinces subject to us. Now, I will take the most important of the territories for which we are exclusively the Legislature—the North-Western Provinces;—and I will take the year in which, judging from the Paper, there has been most North-Western legislation—the year 1867. The amount does not seem to have been very great or serious. I find that in 1867, if Taxing Acts be excluded, the North-West was affected in common with all or other parts of India by an Act repressive of Public Gambling (No. III.); by an Act for the Registration of Printing Presses (No. XXV.); and by five Acts (IV., VII., VIII., X., and XXXIII.); having the most insignificant technical objects. I find that it was exclusively affected by an Act (I.) empowering its Government to levy certain tolls on the Ganges; by an Act (XXII.) for the Regulation of Native Inns; by an Act (XVIII.) giving a legal constitution to the Courts already established in a single district, and by an Act (XXVIII.) confirming the sentences of certain petty Criminal Courts already existing. I find further that, in the same year, 1867, the English Parliament passed 85 Public General Acts applicable to England and Wales, of which one was the Representation of the People Act. The number of Local and Personal

Acts passed in the same year was 188. All this legislation too came, it must be remembered, on the back of a vast mass of statute-law, compared with which all the written law of all India is the merest trifle. Now the population of England and Wales is rather over 20 millions, that of the North-Western Provinces is supposed to be above 30 millions. No trustworthy comparison can be instituted between the two countries; but, regard being had to their condition thirty years ago, it may be doubted whether, in respect of opinions, ideas, habits, and wants, there has not been more change during thirty years in the North-West than in England and Wales.

A third inference which the Paper suggests is, that our legislation scarcely ever interferes, even in the minutest degree, with Private Rights, whether derived from usage or from express law. It has been said by a high authority that the Indian Legislature should confine itself to the amendment of Adjective Law, leaving Substantive Law to the Indian Law Commissioners. It is meant no doubt that the Indian Legislature should only occupy itself, *proprio motu*, with improvements in police, in administration, in the mechanism and procedure of courts of justice. This proposition appears to me a very reasonable one in the main, but it is nearly an exact description of the character of our legislation. We do not meddle with Private Rights; we only create Official Duties. No doubt Act X. of 1865 and Act XV. of 1866 do considerably modify Private Rights, but the first is a chapter and the last a section of the Civil Code framed in England by the Law Commissioners.

The Paper does not of course express the urgency with which the measures which it names are pressed on us by their originators—the Local Governments. My Colleagues are, I believe, aware that the earnestness with which these Governments demand legislation, as absolutely necessary for the discharge of their duties to the people, is sometimes very remarkable. I am very far indeed from believing that, as they are now constituted, they think the Supreme Council precipitate in legislation. I could at this moment name half a dozen instances in which the present Lieutenant-Governors of Bengal and the North-West deem the hesitation of the Government of India in recommending particular enactments to the Legislature unnecessary and unjustifiable.

While it does not seem to me open to doubt that the Government of India is entirely free from the charge of initiating legislation in too great abundance, it may nevertheless be said that we ought to oppose a firmer resistance to the demands of the Local Governments and other authorities for legislative measures. It seems desirable therefore that I should say something of the influences which prompt these Governments, and which constitute the causes of the increase in Indian legislation. I must premise that I do not propose to dwell on causes of great generality. Most people would admit that, for good or for evil, the country is changing rapidly, though not at uniform speed. Opinion, belief, usage, and taste are obviously undergoing more or less modification everywhere. The standard of good government before the minds of officials is constantly shifting, perhaps it is rising. These phenomena are doubtless among the ultimate causes of legislation; but, unless more special causes are assigned, the explanation will never be satisfactory to many minds.

I will first specify a cause which is in itself of a merely formal nature, but which still contributes greatly for the time to the necessity for legislation. This is the effect of the Indian Councils' Act of 1861 upon the system which existed before that date in the Non-Regulation Provinces. It is well known that, in any strict sense of the word, the

P

Executive Government legislated for those Provinces up to 1861. The orders, instructions, circulars, and rules for the guidance of officers which it constantly issued, were, to a certain extent, essentially of a legislative character, but then they were scarcely ever in a legislative form. It is not matter of surprise that this should have been so, for the authority prescribing the rule immediately modified or explained it, if it gave rise to any inconvenience, or was found to be ambiguous. But the system (of which the legality had long been doubted) was destroyed by the Indian Councils' Act. No legislative power now exists in India which is not derived from this Statute; but to prevent a wholesale cancellation of essentially legislative rules, the 25th Section gave the force of law to all rules made previously for Non-Regulation provinces by or under the authority of the Government of India, or of a Lieutenant-Governor. By this provision, an enormous and most miscellaneous mass of rules, clothed to a great extent in general and popular language, was suddenly established as law, and invested with solidity and unchangeableness to a degree which its authors had never contemplated. The difficulty of ascertaining what is law and what is not in the former Non-Regulation Provinces, is really incredible. I have, for instance, been seriously in doubt whether a particular clause of a Circular intended to prescribe a rule or to convey a sarcasm. The necessity for authoritatively declaring rules of this kind, for putting them into precise language, for amending them when their policy is doubted, or when tried by the severer judicial tests now applied to them, they give different results from those intended by their authors, is among the most imperative causes of legislation. Such legislation will, however, diminish as the process of simplifying and declaring these rules goes on, and must ultimately come to a close.

I now come to springs of legislation which appear to increase in activity rather than otherwise. First among these I do not hesitate to place the growing influence of courts of justice and of legal practitioners. Our Courts are becoming more careful of precise rule both at the top and at the bottom. The more careful legal education of the young civilians and of the younger Native judges, diffuses the habit of precision from below; the High Courts, in the exercise of their powers of supervision, are more and more insisting on exactness from above.

An even more powerful influence is the immense multiplication of legal practitioners in the country. I am not now speaking of European practitioners, though their number has greatly increased of late, and though they penetrate much further into the Mofussil than of old. The great addition, however, is to the numbers and influence of the native Bar. Practically a young educated Native, pretending to anything above a clerkship, adopts one of two occupations—either he goes into the service of Government, or he joins the Native Bar. I am told, and I believe it to be true, that the Bar is getting to be more and more preferred to Government service by the educated youth of the country, both on the score of its gainfulness and on the score of its independence.

Now the law of India is at present, and probably will long continue to be, in a state which furnishes opportunity for the suggestion of doubts almost without limit. The older written law of India (the Regulations and earlier Acts) is declared in language which, judged by modern requirements, must be called popular. The authoritative Native treatises on law are so vague that, from many of the dicta embodied by them, almost any conclusion can be drawn. More than that, there are, as the Indian Law Commissioners have pointed out, vast gaps and interspaces in the Substantive Law of India; there are subjects on which no rules exist, and the rules actually applied by the Courts are taken, a good deal at haphazard, from popular text-books of English law. Such a condition of things is a mine of legal difficulty. The Courts are getting ever more rigid in their demand of legal warrant for the actions of all men, officials included. The lawyers who practise before them are getting more and more astute, and render the difficulty of pointing to such legal warrant day by day greater. And unquestionably the Natives of India, living in the constant presence of courts and lawyers, are growing every day less disposed to regard an act or order which they dislike as an unkindly dispensation of Providence, which must be submitted to with all the patience at their command. If British rule is doing nothing else, it is steadily communicating to the Native the consciousness of positive rights, not dependent on opinion or usage, but capable of being actively enforced.

It is not, I think, difficult to see how this state of the law and this condition of the Courts and Bar renders it necessary for the Local Governments, as being responsible for the efficiency of their administration, to press for legislation. The nature of the necessity can best be judged by considering what would be the consequences if there were no legislation, or not enough. A vast variety of points would be unsettled until the highest tribunals had the opportunity of deciding them, and the government of the country would be to a great extent handed over to the High Courts, or to other Courts of Appeal. No court of justice, however, can pay other than incidental regard to considerations of expediency, and the result would be that the country would be governed on principles which have no necessary relation to policy or statesmanship. It is the justification of legislation that it settles difficulties as soon as they arise, and settles them upon considerations which a court of justice is obliged to leave out of sight.

The consequences of having India to be governed by the courts would, in my judgment, be most disastrous. The bolder sort of officials would, I think, go on without regard to legal rule, until something like the deadlock would be reached with which we are about to deal in the Punjab. But the great majority of administrative officials, whether weaker or less reckless, would observe a caution and hesitation for which the doubtful state of the law could always be pleaded. There would, in fact, be a paralysis of administration throughout the country.

The fact established by the Paper, that the duties created by Indian legislation are almost entirely official duties, explains the dislike of legislation which occasionally shows itself here and there in India. I must confess that I have always believed the feeling, so far as it exists, to be official, and to correspond very closely to the repugnance which most lawyers feel to having the most disorderly branch of case-law superseded by the simplest and best drawn of statutes. The truth is, that nobody likes innovations on knowledge which he has once acquired with difficulty. If there was one legislative change which seemed at the time to be more rebelled against than another, it was the supersession of the former Civil Procedure of the Punjab by the Code of Civil Procedure. The Civil Procedure of the Punjab had originally been exceedingly simple, and far better suited to the country than the then existing procedure of the Regulation Provinces. But two years ago it had become so overlaid by explanations and modifications conveyed in Circular orders, that I do not hesitate to pronounce it as uncertain and difficult a body of rules as I ever attempted to study. I can speak with confidence on the point; for I came to India strange both to the Code of Civil Procedure and to the Civil Procedure of the Punjab, and, while the first has always seemed to me nearly the simplest and clearest system of the kind in the world, I must own I never felt sure in any case what was the Punjab rule. The introduction of the Code was, in fact, the merest act of justice to the young generation of Punjab officials, yet the older men spoke of the measure as if some ultra-technical body of law were being forced on a service accustomed to courts of primitive simplicity.

It must, on the other hand, be admitted that, in creating new official duties by legislation, we probably in some degree fetter official discretion. There is no doubt a decay of discretionary administration throughout India; and, indeed, it may be said that in one sense there is now not more, but much less, legislation in the country than formerly; for, strictly speaking, legislation takes place every time a new rule is set to the people, and it may be taken for granted that in earlier days Collectors and Commissioners changed their rules far oftener than does the Legislature at present. The truth is, discretionary government is inconsistent with the existence of regular courts and trained lawyers, and, since these must be tolerated, the proper course seems to me not to indulge in vague condemnation of legislation, but to discover expedients by which its tendency to hamper discretion may be minimised. One of these may be found in the skilful drafting of our laws—in confining them as much as possible to the statement of principles and of well-considered general propositions, and in encumbering them as little as possible with detail. Another may be pointed out in the extension of the wholesale practice of conferring by our Acts on Local Governments or other authorities the power of making rules consistent with the Act—a power in the exercise of which they will be assisted by the Legislative Department under a recent order of His Excellency. Lastly, but principally, we may hope to mitigate the inconveniences of legislation by the simplification of our legislative machinery as applied to those less advanced parts of the country where a large discretion must inevitably be vested in the administrator. The power of easily altering rules when they chafe, and of easily indemnifying officials when they transgress rules in good faith, is urgently needed by us in respect of the wilder territory of India.

While I admit that the abridgment of discretion by written laws is to some extent an evil—though, under the actual circumstances of India, an inevitable evil—I do not admit the proposition which is sometimes advanced that the Natives of India dislike the abridgment of official discretion. This assertion seems to me not only unsupported by any evidence, but to be contrary to all the probabilities. It may be allowed that in some cases discretionary government is absolutely necessary; but why should a people, which measures religious zeal and personal rank and respectability by rigid adherence to usage and custom, have a fancy for rapid changes in the actions of its governors, and prefer a regimen of discretion sometimes coming close upon caprice to a regimen of law? I do not profess to know the Natives of this country as well as others, but if they are to be judged by their writings, they have no such preference. The educated youth of India certainly affect a dislike of many things which they do not care about, and pretend to many tastes which they do not really share; but the repugnance which they invariably profess for discretionary government has always seemed to me genuinely hearty and sincere.

APPENDIX II.[1]

G. L. v. Maurer, Einleitung zur Geschichte der Mark-, Hof-, Dorf-, und Stadt-Verfassung und der öffentlichen Gewalt. München.

G. L. v. Maurer, Geschichte der Dorfverfassung in Deutschland. Erlangen.

G. L. v. Maurer, Geschichte der Frohnhöfe, der Bauernhöfe und der Hofverfassung in Deutschland. Erlangen.

G. L. v. Maurer, Geschichte der Markenverfassung in Deutschland. Erlangen.

G. L. v. Maurer, Geschichte der Städteverfassung in Deutschland. Erlangen.

E. Nasse, Ueber die mittelalterliche Feldgemeinschaft und die Einhegungen des sechszehnten Jahrhunderts in England. Bonn.

G. Landau, Die Territorien in Bezug auf ihre Bildung und ihre Entwicklung. Hamburg.

G. Landau. Das Salgut. Kassel.

Ch. Lette, Die Vertheilung des Grundeigenthums in Zusammenhang mit der Geschichte der Gesetzgebung und den Volkszuständen. Berlin.

N. Kindlinger, Geschichte der deutschen Hörigkeit, insbesondere der sogenannten Leibeigenschaft. Berlin.

W. Gessner, Geschichtliche Entwickelung der gutsherrlichen und bäuerlichen Verhältnisse Deutschlands, oder practische Geschichte der deutschen Hörigkeit. Berlin.

Von Haxthausen, Ueber die Agrarverfassung in Norddeutschland. Berlin.

[1] Vide Preface.

INDEX.

INDEX.

LONDON: PRINTED BY
SPOTTISWOODE AND CO., NEW-STREET SQUARE
AND PARLIAMENT STREET

STANDARD EDITIONS.

AUSTIN'S LECTURES ON GENERAL JURISPRU-
DENCE; or, the Philosophy of Positive Law. *Third Edition*, revised and edited by ROBERT CAMPBELL, Barrister-at-Law. 2 vols. 8vo. 32s.

RAWLINSON'S HISTORY OF HERODOTUS. A
New English Version. Edited, with copious Notes, from the most recent sources of information; and embodying the chief results, historical and ethnographical, which have been obtained in the progress of cuneiform and hieroglyphical discovery. *Second Edition*. With Maps and Woodcuts. 4 vols. 8vo. 48s.

RAWLINSON'S FIVE GREAT MONARCHIES OF
THE ANCIENT WORLD; or, the History, Geography, and Antiquities of Assyria, Babylonia, Chaldæa, Media, and Persia. *Second Edition, revised*. With Maps and Illustrations. 3 vols. 8vo.

GROTE'S HISTORY OF GREECE. From the
Earliest Period to the close of the Generation contemporary with Alexander the Great. *Fifth Edition*. With Portrait, Maps, and Plans. 10 vols. 8vo.

GIBBON'S HISTORY OF THE DECLINE AND
FALL OF THE ROMAN EMPIRE. Edited, with Notes, by WM. SMITH, LL.D. *Fourth Edition*. With Portrait and Maps. 8 vols. 8vo. 60s.

RANKE'S HISTORY OF THE POPES OF ROME
Political and Ecclesiastical. Translated by SARAH AUSTIN. With Preface by DEAN MILMAN. *Fourth Edition*. 3 vols. 8vo. 30s.

HALLAM'S HISTORICAL WORKS. I. History of
England. II. Europe during the Middle Ages. III. Literary History of Europe. 9 vols. 8vo. 96s.

MAHON'S HISTORY OF ENGLAND, from the
Peace of Utrecht to the Peace of Versailles, 1713—1783. *Fourth Edition*. 7 vols. 8vo. 93s.

VON SYBEL'S HISTORY OF EUROPE DURING
THE FRENCH REVOLUTION; drawn up for the most part from Unpublished Papers and Documents in the Secret Archives of Germany. Translated from the third German edition by WALTER C. PERRY. With Index, complete in 4 vols. 8vo. 48s.

DYER'S HISTORY OF MODERN EUROPE; from
the Taking of Constantinople by the Turks, to the Close of the War in the Crimea, 1453—1857. 4 vols. 8vo. 42s.

ROBERTSON'S HISTORY OF THE CHRISTIAN
CHURCH: from the Apostolic Age to the Death of Boniface VIII. A.D. 1122—1303. *Third Edition*. 3 vols. 8vo.

STANDARD EDITIONS.

WORDSWORTH'S GREECE; PICTORIAL, DESCRIPTIVE,
AND HISTORICAL. With an Essay on GREEK ART, by GEORGE SCHARF, F.S.A. With 600 Illustrations. Royal 8vo. 21s.

CROWE AND CAVALCASELLE'S HISTORY OF
PAINTING IN ITALY, the 2nd to the 14th Century, from recent researches in the Archives, as well as from personal inspection of the Works of Art in that country. With 100 Illustrations. 3 vols. 8vo. 63s.

CROWE AND CAVALCASELLE'S HISTORY OF
PAINTING IN NORTH ITALY, VENICE, PADUA, VICENZA, VERONA, FERRARA, MILAN, FRIULI, BRESCHIA, from the 14th to 16th Century. With Illustrations. 2 vols. 8vo. 42s.

FORSYTH'S LIFE AND TIMES OF CICERO;
HIS CHARACTER as a Statesman, Orator, and Friend. With a Selection from his Correspondence and Orations. *Third Edition.* With 20 Illustrations. 8vo. 10s. 6d.

SMILES'S BRITISH ENGINEERS: FROM THE
EARLIEST PERIOD, including the History of Inland Communication in Britain and the INVENTION and INTRODUCTION of the STEAM ENGINE. With 9 Portraits and 350 Illustrations. 4 vols. 8vo. 21s. each.

BIOGRAPHIA JURIDICA; A BIOGRAPHICAL
DICTIONARY OF THE JUDGES OF ENGLAND, FROM THE CONQUEST TO THE PRESENT TIME, 1066—1870. *New Edition.* By EDWARD FOSS. (800 pp.) 8vo. 21s.

KING'S CATHEDRALS OF ENGLAND; a CONCISE
HISTORY of each SEE, with BIOGRAPHICAL NOTICES of the BISHOPS. With 250 Illustrations. 4 vols. Post 8vo. 58s.

THE SOUTHERN DIVISION.—WINCHESTER, SALISBURY, EXETER, WELLS, ROCHESTER, CANTERBURY, AND CHICHESTER. With 120 Illustrations. 2 vols. 24s.

THE EASTERN DIVISION.—OXFORD, PETERBOROUGH, LINCOLN, NORWICH, AND ELY. With 90 Illustrations. 18s.

THE WESTERN DIVISION.—BRISTOL, GLOUCESTER, WORCESTER, HEREFORD, AND LICHFIELD. With 50 Illustrations. 16s.

THE WELSH CATHEDRALS.—LLANDAFF, BANGOR, ST. ASAPH, AND ST. DAVID'S. With Illustrations.

' The manuals, histories, descriptions, essays, and so forth, of and upon mediæval architecture are innumerable, and yet a systematic portable account of all the English Cathedrals, compiled in the terms of modern architectural science, remained a desideratum. This is full of very valuable information, architectural, archæological, historical, and artistic.
SATURDAY REVIEW.

JOHN MURRAY, Albemarle Street.

Lightning Source UK Ltd.
Milton Keynes UK
UKHW020632130422
401507UK00005B/330